BALANCING LITERACY

A BALANCED APPROACH TO READING AND WRITING INSTRUCTION

Written by

Caroline A. Coleman

Editor: Carla Hamaguchi
Illustrator: Darcy Tom
Cover Illustrator: Reggie Holladay
Designers: Moonhee Pak and Terri Lamadrid
Cover Designer: Moonhee Pak
Art Director: Tom Cochrane
Project Director: Carolea Williams

Table of Contents

Introduction

What are the components of a balanced literacy program? How do you incorporate all of them into your school day? Which types of activities should you use to improve your students' reading and writing skills? *Balancing Literacy* answers these questions and many more.

You've heard of phonics instruction, whole language, the writing process, and guided reading. Several issues and controversies surround the usage of some of these approaches to teaching literacy. Rather than try to identify which method is the best, a balanced literacy program incorporates several components, which together comprise an effective daily reading/language instructional program.

Each component helps students with some aspect of the reading and writing process. The Reading and Writing sections explain these components and suggest activities that reinforce each component. The components are presented separately to help you gain a better understanding of each one, but remember that an effective literacy program incorporates all the components.

After you have an understanding of each component, plan to effectively incorporate all the components into your daily schedule. Use some of the ideas and suggestions provided in the first part of the book, or turn to the Balancing Your Literacy Program section (pages 70–110) to find out about three different teaching methods that incorporate several components. Learn how to implement Reader's and Writer's Workshop, Literature Circles, and Literacy Centers and review the sample schedule for each method. This section also features an explanation of how each schedule incorporates the literacy components.

Recording and observing each student's progress is an integral part of any literacy program. There are many forms of assessment, each lending something a little different. Choosing the types of assessment to use depends on many factors. Use the information and reproducibles in the Assessment section (pages 111–125) to decide which methods of assessment will work best in your classroom.

Creating a balanced literacy program will take time. Experiment with the various possibilities presented in this book until you find the right match for your teaching style and the needs of your students.

What Is a Balanced Literacy Program?

The following list includes the components of a balanced literacy program and explains how each component helps students with the reading and writing process:

Modeled Reading: Teacher reads aloud selections to students
- provides an adult model of fluent reading
- develops a sense of story
- enriches concept and vocabulary development
- encourages prediction
- fosters a love and enthusiasm for reading

Shared Reading: Teacher and students read text together
- develops a sense of story or content
- promotes reading strategies
- increases comprehension
- develops fluency
- expands students' vocabulary

Guided Reading: Teacher works with a group of students similar in strengths and needs and provides instruction through mini-lessons
- promotes reading strategies
- increases comprehension
- encourages independent reading
- strengthens students' thinking skills
- allows the teacher to work with individual groups of students on specific reading skills

Independent Reading: Students read independently
- supports writing development
- extends experiences with a variety of written texts
- promotes reading for enjoyment and information
- develops fluency
- fosters self-confidence as students read familiar and new text

Modeled and Shared Writing: Teacher and students collaborate to write text; teacher acts as scribe
- develops concepts about print
- develops writing strategies
- supports reading development
- provides a model for a variety of writing styles
- produces text that students can read independently

Interactive Writing: Teacher and students compose text together using a "shared pen" technique in which students do some of the writing
- provides opportunities to plan and construct text
- increases spelling knowledge
- produces written language resources in the classroom

Guided Writing: Teacher works with a group of students similar in strengths and needs and provides instruction through mini-lessons
- models brainstorming of ideas
- provides students with guidance while learning the writing process
- provides an audience for the written word

Independent Writing: Students write independently
- strengthens text sequence
- develops an understanding of multiple uses of writing
- supports reading development
- develops writing strategies

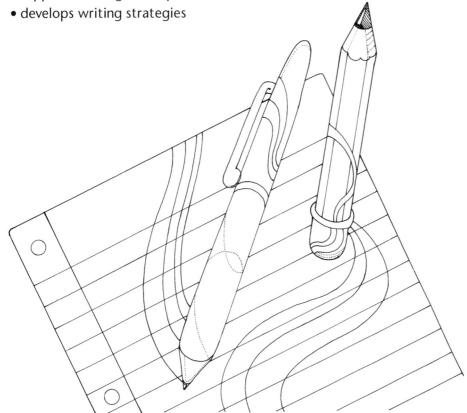

Reading

Teaching reading is one of a teacher's most essential—not to mention challenging—tasks. Provide students with ample amounts of reading opportunities on a daily basis. Have students read independently or with a partner. Guide students in their reading by offering them assistance in a small-group setting. Also be sure to set aside time each day to read to students. This will help enhance their listening and comprehension skills.

Provide a comfortable and inviting area in your classroom where students can read books of their choice. Couches, pillows, or beanbags add a cozy feeling to the area. Display books and novels of various genres in the area. Magazines, comic books, and class-made books can also be housed there.

Reading doesn't just occur in books. Display charts around the room for students to read and refer to. Post directions and instructions for activities as well as reference charts and notes.

The following section presents various components and methods of teaching reading to your students. Incorporate all the reading components into your daily schedule to provide students with a variety of reading experiences.

MODELED READING

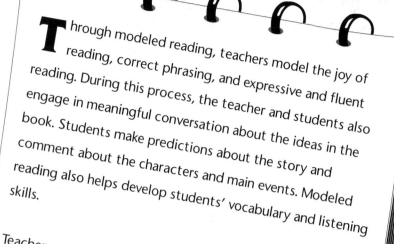

Through modeled reading, teachers model the joy of reading, correct phrasing, and expressive and fluent reading. During this process, the teacher and students also engage in meaningful conversation about the ideas in the book. Students make predictions about the story and comment about the characters and main events. Modeled reading also helps develop students' vocabulary and listening skills.

Teacher read-alouds are opportunities for modeled reading. Choose books from a variety of genres and authors to read aloud to your class. These books can relate to a current topic of study or simply be class favorites. Take at least 10–15 minutes each day to read aloud to students. At the end of each session, have students summarize the story or chapter content and make predictions as to what will happen next. Foster your students' love for literature by sharing the read-aloud books listed below.

SUGGESTED READ-ALOUD BOOKS

Bridge to Terabithia by Katherine Paterson
(HarperCollins)
A Newbery Award winner about a boy who becomes a close friend of a new girl in school and suffers agony after her accidental death.

Charlotte's Web by E. B. White (HarperCollins)
Classic, whimsical barnyard fable about a spider who saves the life of a pig.

The Cricket in Times Square by George Selden
(Farrar, Straus, & Giroux)
A Connecticut cricket is transported in a picnic basket to New York's Times Square.

Danny, the Champion of the World by Roald Dahl
(Econo-Clad Books)
Nine-year-old Danny helps his father on a poaching expedition to wealthy Mr. Hazell's woods.

Dear Mr. Henshaw by Beverly Cleary
(William Morrow & Co.)
A Newbery Award winner about a boy who pours out his problems in letters to a writer he greatly admires.

Freckle Juice by Judy Blume (Yearling)
A gullible 2nd grader pays fifty cents for a recipe to grow freckles.

Frindle by Andrew Clements (Aladdin)
Nick, a champion time-waster, faces the challenge of his life when confronted with the toughest teacher in the school, Mrs. Granger.

From the Mixed-up Files of Mrs. Basil E. Frankweiler by E. L. Konigsburg (Atheneum)
A Newbery Award winner about a 12-year-old girl and her younger brother who elude security guards and live for a week in New York's Metropolitan Museum of Art.

Holes by Louis Sachar (Farrar, Straus, & Giroux)
This Newbery Award winner follows the internment of a boy in a juvenile detention camp who is forced by the warden to dig holes to uncover an outlaw's hidden treasure.

How to Eat Fried Worms by Thomas Rockwell (Yearling)
Billy takes on a bet—he will eat 15 worms a day. His family and friends help devise ways to cook them.

The Hundred Dresses by Eleanor Estes (Harcourt Brace)
A little Polish girl in an American school finally wins acceptance by her classmates.

In the Year of the Boar and Jackie Robinson by Bette Bao Lord (HarperCollins)
The story of a Chinese girl who leaves China to join her father in New York in 1947.

James and the Giant Peach by Roald Dahl (Knopf)
James is unhappy living with his mean aunts until a magic potion produces an enormous peach, which becomes a home for him.

Maniac Magee by Jerry Spinelli (Little, Brown & Co.)
A Newbery Award winner about a homeless boy who confronts racism in a small town.

Mrs. Frisby and the Rats of Nimh by Robert O'Brien (Atheneum)
This Newbery Award winner is about a group of rats, made literate and given human intelligence, who escape from their laboratory to start their own community.

Sarah, Plain and Tall by Patricia MacLachlan (HarperCollins)
A Newbery Award winner about two children on a prairie who wait for the arrival of their new stepmother.

The Secret Garden by Frances Hodgson Burnett (HarperCollins)
Three children find a secret garden and make it bloom again; the garden, in turn, changes the children.

Tales of a Fourth Grade Nothing by Judy Blume (E. P. Dutton)
The story of Peter Hatcher's trials and tribulations, most of which are caused by his two-year-old pesky brother, Fudge.

The View from Saturday by E. L. Konigsburg (Atheneum)
A story about a group of sixth graders chosen to be on the Academic Bowl team.

Walk Two Moons by Sharon Creech (HarperCollins)
A Newbery Award winner about a 13-year-old girl journeying to find her mother.

SHARED READING

Shared reading provides an enjoyable reading experience for students. It is a supportive reading situation that enables them to feel secure. The students are involved and contribute whenever they are able. Through effective modeling by the teacher, students can read text of a more difficult nature than they would normally read. Shared reading is useful for encouraging prediction in reading, informally introducing print conventions, and teaching sight vocabulary.

Shared reading sessions can be conducted as a whole-group, small-group, or one-on-one activity. Refer to the suggested shared reading sequence to help you plan these sessions. The text being shared must be accessible to all students, so for a whole-group activity, use reading materials in large print, including Big Books, charts, overhead transparencies, and sentence strips in pocket charts. Use a variety of print resources, including fiction and nonfiction books, poetry, student-written materials, or text from other subject areas.

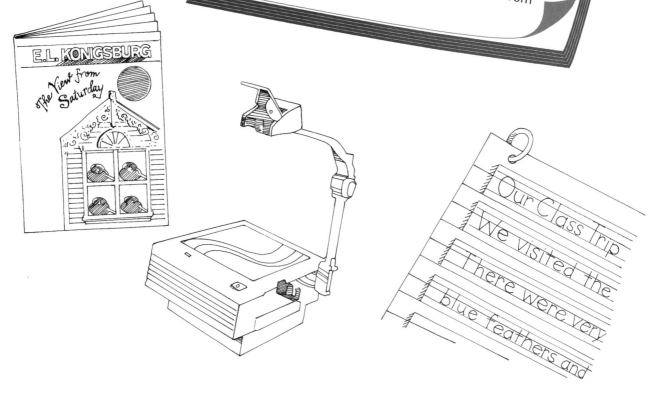

Suggested Shared Reading Sequence

1. Decide on the focus.
   - Read a predictable story.
   - Introduce a new or specific author or illustrator.
   - Introduce a new topic or theme.
   - Explore a new genre.
   - Demonstrate specific reading strategies or skills that students need to practice.
2. Select an appropriate book.
   - Does it support the focus?
   - Is it interesting?
   - Does it provide a sufficient challenge for the students?
3. Discuss the text.
   - Talk about the title, author, illustrator, and front and back covers.
   - Prompt students to predict the theme.
   - Read the text with few interruptions. Encourage participation and prediction, but not to the detriment of the story line.
4. Reread the text.
   - Have students participate in reading. Invite them to recall vocabulary, ideas, and information and observe and demonstrate reading strategies and language conventions.
5. Respond to the text.
   - Have students respond through discussion, writing, retelling, drama, role play, arts and crafts, and student-made books.
6. Share responses.
   - Invite students to share their responses. Sharing provides the chance for students to develop oral-language and listening skills.

Responding to the Text

The following activities present various ways for students to respond to a shared reading text. Explain and model how to complete the reproducible activity sheets. Then, have students independently complete an activity sheet. These sheets can also serve as an assessment tool to check for students' reading comprehension.

STORY OCTAGON

Copy the Story Octagon reproducible (page 12) onto an overhead transparency. Discuss with students the meaning of story elements (e.g., characters, setting, problem, and solution). Read a shared reading text with the class. Then, ask for student responses to complete the Story Octagon transparency. This activity helps improve student comprehension and reviews the parts of the story.

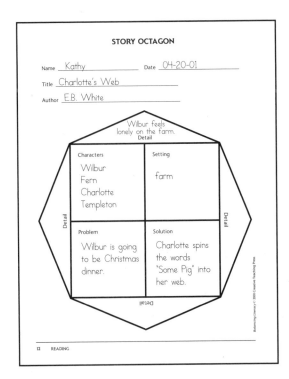

TRIANGLE-GRAM

Read aloud two books on a similar subject or that have similar elements. Have each student complete the Triangle-gram reproducible (page 13). Ask students to write the differences between the stories in separate triangles. Have them record similarities in the space where the two triangles overlap.

CHAIN OF EVENTS

Copy the Chain of Events reproducible (page 14) onto an overhead transparency, or make a paper copy for each student. Read a book with the class, and discuss the major events in the story. Write the events in sequential order, one per ring, or have students fill in their copy of the reproducible.

CHARACTERIZATION HOUSE

Read a book with the class. Give each student a copy of the Characterization House reproducible (page 15). Have students pick one character and one event involving that character from the story. Have students write the book title and author's name. Encourage them to write the correct response to each question.

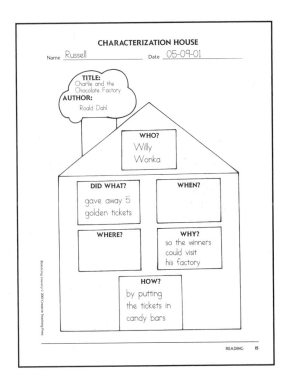

STORY OCTAGON

Name _____ Date _____

Title _____

Author _____

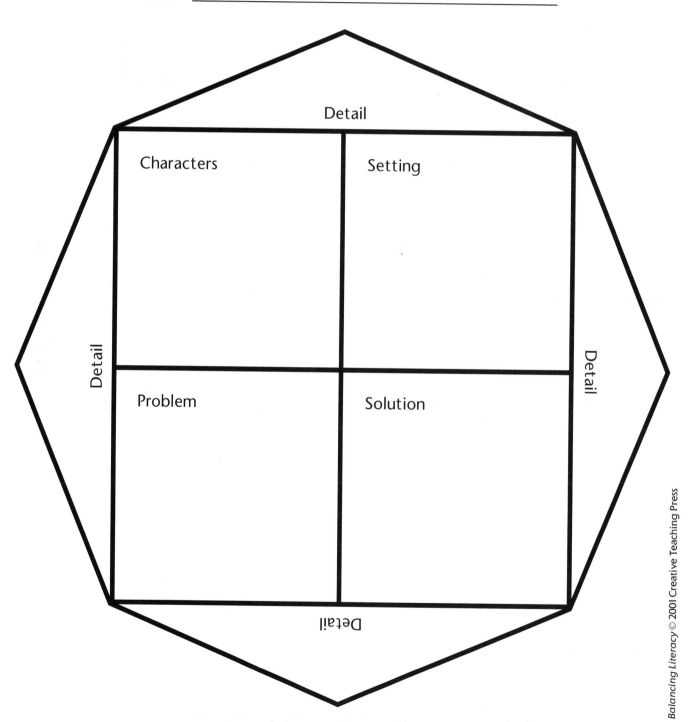

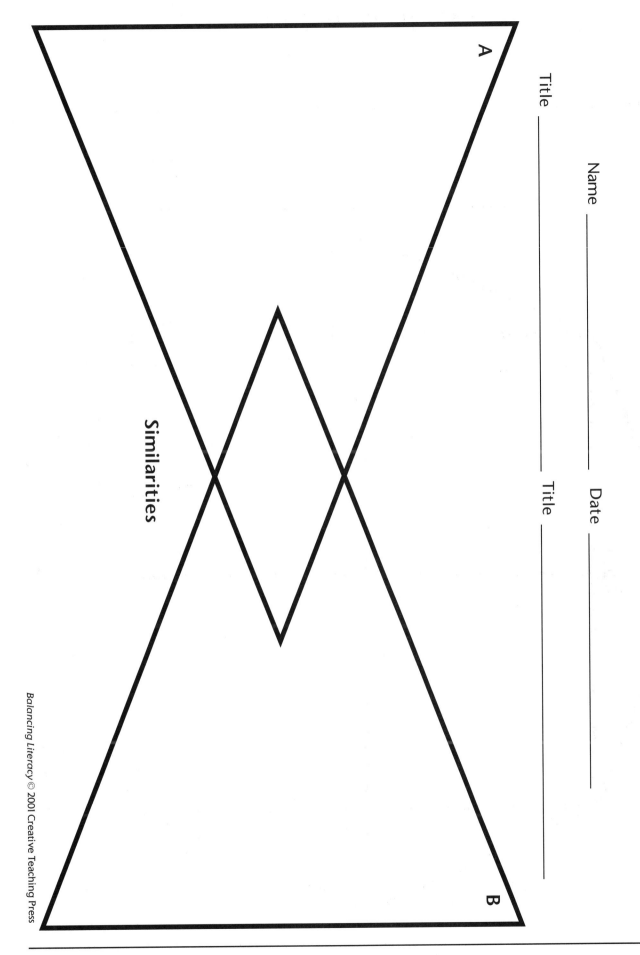

TRIANGLE-GRAM

A

Title _____

Name _____

Similarities

Date _____

Title _____

B

CHAIN OF EVENTS

Name _____

Title _____

Date _____

Directions: List the major events of the story in sequential order from beginning to end. Record one event in each chain link.

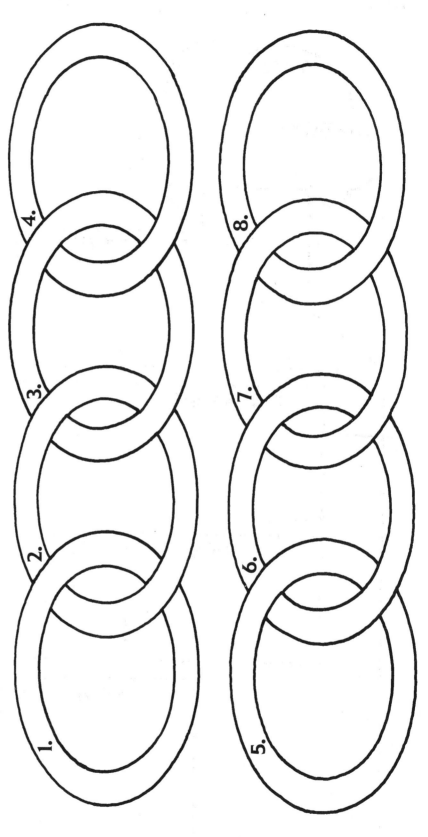

Balancing Literacy © 2001 Creative Teaching Press

CHARACTERIZATION HOUSE

Name _____ Date _____

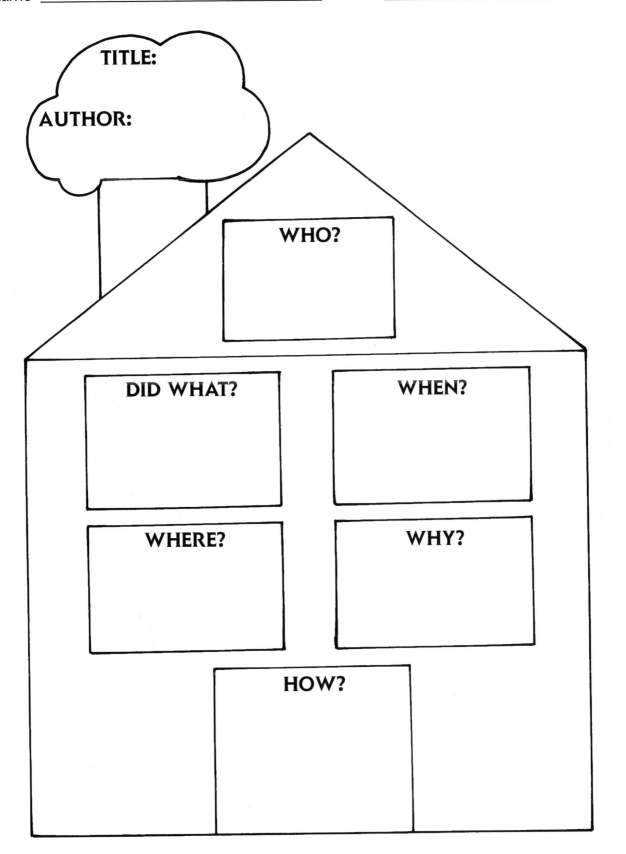

TITLE:

AUTHOR:

WHO?

DID WHAT?

WHEN?

WHERE?

WHY?

HOW?

GUIDED READING

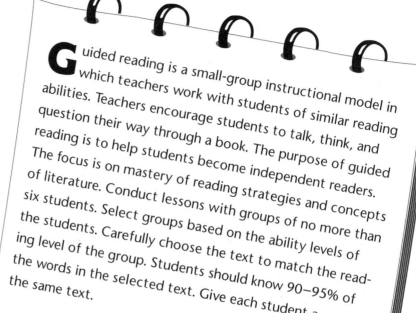

G uided reading is a small-group instructional model in which teachers work with students of similar reading abilities. Teachers encourage students to talk, think, and question their way through a book. The purpose of guided reading is to help students become independent readers. The focus is on mastery of reading strategies and concepts of literature. Conduct lessons with groups of no more than six students. Select groups based on the ability levels of the students. Carefully choose the text to match the reading level of the group. Students should know 90–95% of the words in the selected text. Give each student a copy of the same text.

Guided reading can be done in a variety of ways. Choose the format that best meets your students' need. Some students need more teacher guidance, some need to focus on reading cues, and others may need to focus on literary elements. This section presents a general format to give you a better understanding of how to include guided reading in your classroom.

CREATING GUIDED READING GROUPS

There are several reasons why it is best to group students according to ability level. Students will have the opportunity to work on skills that address specific areas of need. Also, a mini-lesson on a specific skill is more meaningful in a homogeneous group, and students participate in the lesson with more confidence and comfort. Ability grouping also allows you to better plan lessons that target the individual needs of each group. This approach also affords a great deal of flexibility because you can move students to new groups based on their academic performance.

Guided Reading Groups

Group 1
Derek
Camryn
Tyler
Kiana
Traci
Darin

Group 2
Gail
Glenn
Corey
Jan
Tiffany
Ken

Group 3
Ryan

Group 4
Ashley
Eric
Arielle

Suggested Guided Reading Sequence

Use the following outline to help you plan your guided reading sessions.

1. Introduce the book.
   - Introduce the title of the book. Discuss the cover illustrations with the group.
   - Discuss unfamiliar concepts. Determine the students' prior knowledge and what they need to know to successfully read the book. Introduce any new information.
2. Read the book.
   - Ask questions to encourage students to make predictions.
   - Guide students to silently read a selection to find and confirm the literary elements.
3. Reread the book.
   - Have students read the story independently and silently.
   - Have students respond in response journals. This can be done on the following day.

4. Initiate class discussion.
   - Invite students to share their response journal entries, discuss literary elements, discuss thoughts and feelings about the story, or retell the story.
5. Present a mini-lesson.
   - Discuss literary elements, language structures, or reading strategies. Introduce or review concepts that occur in or relate to the story.
6. Assign an extension activity.
   - Lead a group discussion based on reactions to response journals. Have students do a literature-related activity.
7. Prepare for the next session.
   - Introduce a new chapter or story for the next day's reading.

Guided Reading Organization

Guided reading is need based; spend more time with students who have the greatest reading needs. Because guided reading is focused tightly on the needs of each group, plan for about 20 minutes of instruction per day. Depending on the number of groups you have, you may not be able to meet with every group each day. You may only need to meet with one group once or twice a week, whereas you may need to meet with another group three times a week. Meet with higher-need groups at least three times a week for consistency. Here is a sample guided reading schedule.

Group 1 = lowest reading ability
Group 2 = low to average reading ability
Group 3 = average reading ability
Group 4 = above average reading ability

Monday	Tuesday	Wednesday	Thursday	Friday
Groups 1, 2, and 3	Groups 1, 2, and 4	Groups 1 and 2	Groups 1, 3, and 4	Work with groups as needed.

INDEPENDENT READING

During independent reading, students individually select and read materials appropriate to their reading abilities. Independent reading develops students' reading abilities and appreciation for reading, promotes fluency, and challenges students to become independent problem solvers.

One way to incorporate independent reading into your class schedule is to have a daily Sustained Silent Reading (S.S.R.) period in your class. During this time, students and teachers silently read books or materials of their choice. The classroom atmosphere needs to be serene and conducive to uninterrupted involvement with print. The length of the period depends on your class. Start out with a 15-minute period of S.S.R. and gradually increase that time throughout the school year. Do not require book reports or reading logs from students at this time. The goal of S.S.R. is to develop a lifelong interest and enjoyment in reading.

A student reading log, parent information letter, and list of literary genres are provided to encourage student independent reading at school and home.

READING LOG

As a follow-up to S.S.R., have students record the title, number of pages, and genre of each book that they read on a copy of the Reading Log (page 22). Staple together several reading log sheets to make a reading log for each student. Have students take their log home each week to record any reading done at home. Collect the reading logs at the end of each week to keep track of their reading. Set a reading goal for the class. When the class reaches the goal, celebrate with a party, give students bookmarks, or invite an author or a parent volunteer to do a read-aloud.

PARENTS AS PARTNERS

Tell parents how important it is for them to read to their children and encourage independent reading at home. Have each student fill out a Parents as Partners Letter (page 23) and take it home to their parents. The letter explains several reading strategies and gives parents suggestions to improve their child's reading.

Genres

Encourage students to read a wide range of reading materials from a variety of genres. Challenge them to read at least one book from each of the following genres during the school year. Have them record each selection on their reading log (page 22).

FICTION

Tells about imaginary people and events

- Folklore
  Handed down by word of mouth through generations; includes folktales, fables, tall tales, legends, and myths (e.g., *The Boy Who Cried Wolf*)
- Fantasy
  Make-believe stories about events that could not happen in real life (e.g., *The Three Little Pigs*)
- Fairy Tale
  Contains some magical being, such as elves or fairies (e.g., *Beauty and the Beast*)
- Humor or Comedy
  Has a funny and amusing quality (e.g., *Green Eggs and Ham* by Dr. Seuss)
- Mystery
  Contains a hidden secret that is revealed in the end (e.g., *Cam Jansen and the Mystery of the Stolen Diamonds* by David A. Adler)
- Drama
  Written to be acted out by actors and actresses (e.g., a play or puppet show)
- Adventure
  Action-packed story that usually contains heroes and villains (e.g., *Treasure Island* by Robert Louis Stevenson)
- Science Fiction
  Describes adventures in places such as outer space and the world of the future (e.g., *A Wrinkle in Time* by Madeleine L'Engle)
- Historical Fiction
  Describes how people lived during a particular time (e.g., *Little House on the Prairie* by Laura Ingalls Wilder)

NONFICTION

Tells about real people and events

- Biography
  Introduces readers to the lives of important people (e.g., *A Picture Book of Martin Luther King, Jr.* by David A. Adler)
- Expository/Informative
  Introduces readers to the world of learning through facts and information (e.g., science or social studies informational books)

READING LOG

Name _____ Date _____

Title of Book	Number of Pages	Genre

Balancing Literacy © 2001 Creative Teaching Press

PARENTS AS PARTNERS LETTER

Date _____

Dear _____ ,

My teacher, _____ , says in
order for me to learn my best, we need to work together. This is
a list of suggestions that my teacher wants me to share with you
to help me practice reading at home.

1. I should have a variety of books to read. I could visit the
   public library or even get a book as a present.
2. I could check out or subscribe to a children's magazine
   (e.g., *3-2-1 Contact*, *Sports Illustrated for Kids*).
3. I should read everything! This includes the grocery list, road
   signs, baseball cards, and recipes.
4. Allow me to choose the books that I want to read. This way
   I will enjoy reading more.
5. I could read to you or others. I can also read by myself
   or listen to you read a story to me. Let's have a family
   reading time.
6. I can use my finger or a bookmark as a pointer or guide while
   I am reading.
7. As I read, I should predict what will happen next.
8. Encourage me to use the following reading strategies:
   • Look at the pictures for clues.
   • Ask, "What word would make sense based on the story's
     meaning?"
   • Reread the sentence(s).
   • Ask, "Have you seen this word somewhere else?"
   • Pronounce the letter sounds or word parts.

Thank you so much for helping me with my reading!

Your child,

_____

Balancing Literacy © 2001 Creative Teaching Press

READING STRATEGIES

Reading strategies represent actions students can take when they come across an obstacle during reading. Because the ability to use reading strategies is an applied skill, teach them within the context of an actual reading situation. This allows you to teach specific reading strategies as well as overall reading skills. Students who master these strategies are able to consciously monitor and modify their own reading process.

Teach students the reading strategies listed below, and model how to apply them properly. Copy the graphic reminder from the Helping Hand reproducible (page 25) on chart paper, and display it, or photocopy the reproducible for individual use. The goal is for students to use self-monitoring strategies to become better independent readers.

A. MEANING (SEMANTICS)

What is the meaning of the text? Does it make sense?
Students use context clues. Students read the text again and think about what would make sense. Sometimes the first letter is given to point out that while many words work with that same first letter—only some make sense.
Example: My mother and f_____ fixed me dinner. father, fast, fox. Student concludes that only father makes sense.

Students use picture clues to help decode the text.

B. STRUCTURE (SYNTACTICS)

Does this sound correct?
Students check to see if the word makes sense with the story's grammar and arrangement of words.
Example: I found my _____ hat on the floor. Prompt the student to reread the sentence and think about what would sound right.

C. VISUAL (GRAPHOPHONICS)

Does this look correct?
Students take the word apart. They identify the different types of word chunks and pronounce the sounds these chunks make when they're together.
Example: flight—/fl/ -ight—flight

Have you seen this word before? Does this word remind you of another word you already know (e.g., prettier, pretty)? Students rely on prior knowledge to read text.
Example: The student previously read the word in a story or on a word wall in the classroom.

HELPING HAND

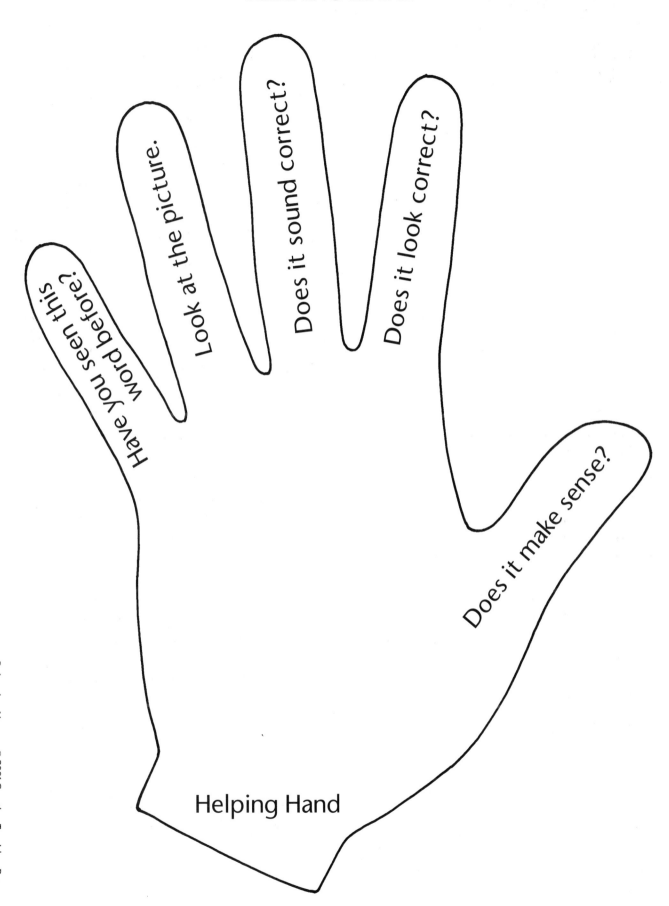

Have you seen this word before?

Look at the picture.

Does it sound correct?

Does it look correct?

Does it make sense?

Helping Hand

Writing

In order for students to become proficient writers, they need to write frequently. They can write lists, notes, questions, conversations, paragraphs, memories, stories, reports, poems, and more. There are several approaches to teaching writing. This section explores different teaching methods and provides sample activities to incorporate into your writing program. Choose the techniques that work best for your class. Just remember that your students will benefit from writing on a daily basis.

Students in a successful writing program

- write for a purpose (e.g., article for a school newspaper)
- practice all stages of the writing process (i.e., prewriting, drafting, revising, editing, and publishing)
- display and share their work with other students, teachers, parents (e.g., bulletin boards, Author's Chair)
- write for communication purposes (e.g., pen pals, dialogue journals)
- perform peer editing
- have ample materials and resources to assist them with their writing (e.g., word wall, writing folders)
- engage in a wide variety of writing activities
- meet with the teacher for writing conferences
- use different writing styles (e.g., narrative, descriptive, persuasive, informative, expressive, imaginative)

MODELED AND SHARED WRITING

Modeled writing is writing that the teacher does in front of the class. While writing, talk about the writing and discuss the process and the decisions that a writer makes. Model writing techniques such as how to choose a topic or when to include punctuation marks. Write on chart paper, the chalkboard, or an overhead projector so the text will be visible to all students. Have students give input regarding the content and it becomes a shared writing lesson. Use the following activities to implement modeled and shared writing in your classroom.

CLASS NEWS

Ask students to think about the things that they did in school that day. Choose one of the responses, and write about it on chart paper. As you write, point out when you use capital letters, punctuation marks, and any other writing rules that may arise. Ask students how to spell some of the words as you write them. Have students read the final sentence or paragraph. Invite one or two students to be illustrators, and have them draw a picture for the text. Save the completed pages, and staple them together to make a book titled *Our Class News* that can be read during S.S.R. or by classroom visitors. For a variation, write about something that occurred in the life of one of the students (e.g., the birth of a new sibling).

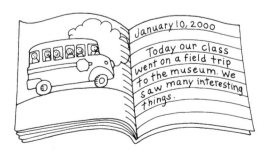

HOT WORDS

Show students how to "spice" up their writing with "hot words." Make an enlarged copy of the Word Thermometer reproducible (page 28). Tell students that some words are overused and not very exciting and that usually you can find a "hotter" word to use. Write the overused word (e.g., *said*) near the bottom of the thermometer. Ask students to tell you different words that mean the same as *said*. Write one of the words (e.g., *remarked*) above *said,* and say Remarked *is a hotter word than* said. Then, choose another word (e.g., *exclaimed*), say Exclaimed *is even hotter than* remarked, and write it above *remarked*. Continue in this manner until you have several variations of the word *said*. Complete a thermometer for other

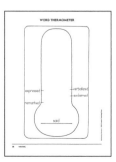

overused words as needed. Compile completed sheets into a class book titled *Hot Words*. Have students refer to the book every time they need a hot word.

WORD THERMOMETER

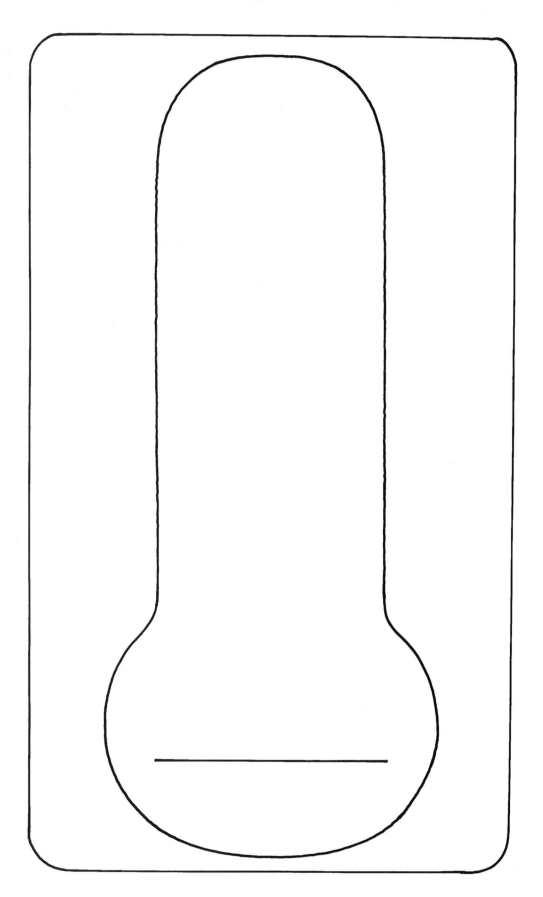

INTERACTIVE WRITING

Interactive writing is a teacher-guided group or one-on-one activity designed to teach students about the writing process and about how written language works. The teacher and students write meaningful text together, or "share the pen." Have individual students write words or sentences, and then fill in the blanks. This procedure builds upon what students have learned from class participation, shared reading, and language experiences. Students take an active role in the writing process as you scaffold the learning. Scaffolding implies that what students can do with help, they can eventually do on their own. Scaffold each task by engaging students in appropriate instructional interactions (e.g., asking open-ended questions, encouraging students to verbalize their thinking process). Text created during interactive writing is intended to be read repeatedly by students, so the text should adhere to standard conventions of spelling and grammar. While creating text, teach correct spelling, punctuation, capitalization, and other writing conventions.

TEACH PARAGRAPH WRITING

Display chart paper on an easel. Discuss with the class the components of a paragraph (e.g., topic sentence, supporting details, concluding statement). Ask for volunteers to provide a topic sentence. Have the class choose one of the topic sentences, and ask a volunteer to write that sentence on the chart paper. As the volunteer writes, comment on spelling and/or grammar conventions as necessary. Encourage the writer to make any necessary corrections. Ask for another volunteer to write the next sentence in the paragraph. Ask if the sentence supports the topic sentence.

Continue in this manner to complete the paragraph. Label the components of the paragraph on the chart paper. Hang the paper on the wall for students to refer to when they are writing independently.

GUIDED WRITING

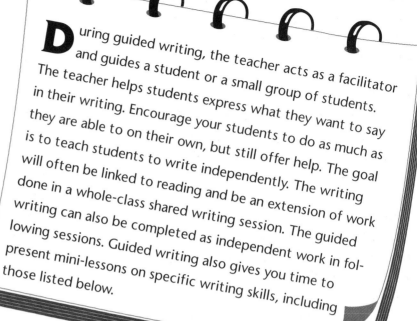

During guided writing, the teacher acts as a facilitator and guides a student or a small group of students. The teacher helps students express what they want to say in their writing. Encourage your students to do as much as they are able to on their own, but still offer help. The goal is to teach students to write independently. The writing will often be linked to reading and be an extension of work done in a whole-class shared writing session. The guided writing can also be completed as independent work in following sessions. Guided writing also gives you time to present mini-lessons on specific writing skills, including those listed below.

SUGGESTED MINI-LESSON TOPICS

- use of punctuation marks
- how to write a topic sentence
- how to edit writing
- how to write a paragraph
- when to capitalize letters
- fluency
- types of sentence structure (e.g., simple, compound)

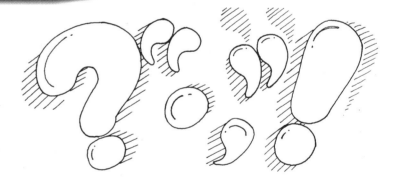

GUIDED WRITING SESSION — BIOGRAPHICAL REPORT

1. Use resources (e.g., encyclopedia, Internet) to gather information on a famous person (e.g., Martin Luther King Jr.). Write important information and dates on a sheet of paper.

2. Make a copy of the information page for each student. Make an overhead transparency of the Research Information Grid (page 32), and make a copy for each student. Tell students that they will write a report on Martin Luther King Jr. based on information they will read.

3. Give each student a grid. Ask students *What are some of the important things that readers would want to know about Martin Luther King Jr.?* Based on their answers, prompt students to come up with subtopics for the report (e.g., childhood, education, work, family).

4. Write the subtopics in the top row of the transparency grid, and have students write them on their individual grid.

5. Give each student a copy of the information page. Have students read the information and keep in mind the subtopics of the report as they read.

6. Have students put the information page aside, and ask what facts they remember and what subtopic each fact should be listed under. Write their responses on the class grid, and have students write them on their individual grid. Fill in any important information that the class did not mention.

7. Tape a large piece of chart paper to the chalkboard, and give each student a piece of lined paper. Guide the class through changing the notes in the grid into sentence and paragraph form. Ask the class which subtopic would make the best beginning. Ask for a volunteer to generate a topic sentence to begin the paragraph and write that sentence on the chart paper. Have students copy the sentence onto their own paper.

8. Continue in this manner until you have a finished product, or have students complete the rest of the report on their own.

9. Proofread the finished product with the class.

Show the class how and where to conduct their research (e.g., encyclopedias, Internet). Now students should be able to research a topic and compose a report on their own. In the sample lesson, students only used one source to research the topic. Explain to students that when they write their own reports they will find information from at least two sources. If some students are still unable to do so, plan to conduct another guided writing lesson with those students on another day.

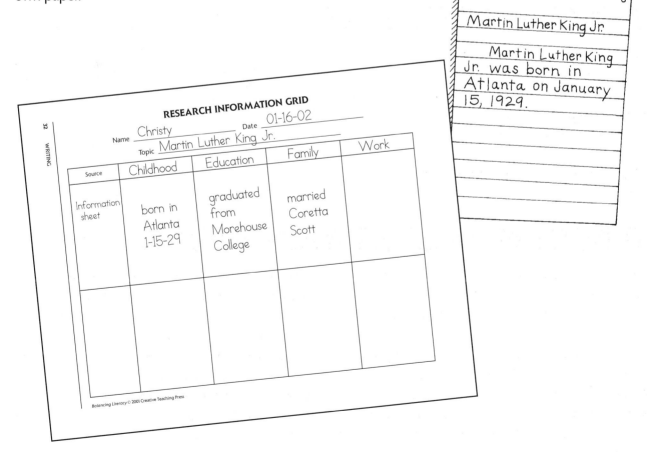

RESEARCH INFORMATION GRID

Name _____ Date _____

Topic _____

Source		

Balancing Literacy © 2001 Creative Teaching Press

INDEPENDENT WRITING

Independent writing is generated by students and requires little teacher support. Students write their own messages and stories, using known words and constructing spelling of unknown words. Students refer to the print around them on word walls, on charts, in dictionaries, or on the computer.

Independent writing provides opportunities for open-ended writing experiences, such as writing letters, making invitations, journal writing, creative writing, and making lists. Students also learn to use strategies that were introduced in previous writing lessons.

By observing students during independent writing, you can better plan for mini-lessons and writing tips to teach during shared, modeled, or interactive writing.

There are several activities explained in this book that provide students the opportunity to write independently. See pages 76–88 for an explanation of how students write independently during Writer's Workshop. Set up a Post Office Center (page 109) and encourage students to write letters to one another, or have a Writing Center (page 107) where they can write stories, poems, and plays.

WRITING PROCESS

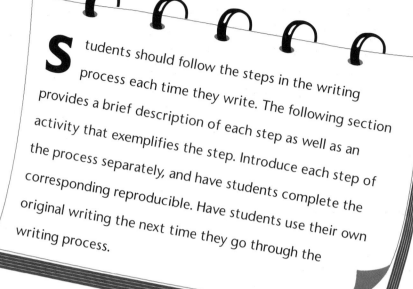

Students should follow the steps in the writing process each time they write. The following section provides a brief description of each step as well as an activity that exemplifies the step. Introduce each step of the process separately, and have students complete the corresponding reproducible. Have students use their own original writing the next time they go through the writing process.

STEP 1: PREWRITING

Have students choose a topic and then brainstorm (e.g., create a cluster, list related details), draw pictures, or read a book to generate writing ideas. These activities can be done by the whole class, by small groups, in pairs, or independently. Next, have students read over their details and cross off any that are off the topic. They may choose the title of their story at this stage.

- Prewriting Practice
  Have students complete the My Best Birthday Ever reproducible (page 36).

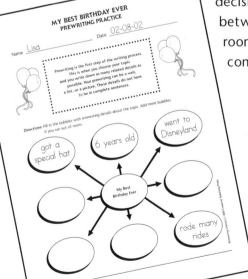

STEP 2: DRAFTING

Have students use their prewriting details to write complete sentences. Encourage them to get all of their ideas down on paper. It is not necessary at this step for students to spend a lot of time making spelling and punctuation decisions. Have students skip spaces between each line on the page to leave room for any necessary revisions and comments.

- Drafting Practice
  Have students complete the My Best Birthday Ever reproducible (page 37). Have them use their prewriting sheet to complete this page.

STEP 3: REVISING

Have students reread their story and make necessary changes by adding, deleting, or reorganizing the material. Remind them to check for correct sequencing (beginning, middle, end), add interesting details, use descriptive language, and delete details that may be off the topic. Also, ask them to fix run-on sentences, combine short simple sentences using transitional words (e.g., and, but, because), and check for use of varied sentence types. Teach and model the use of proofreading symbols with the Editing Marks reproducible (page 86).

• Revising Practice
Have students read the Tooth Story reproducible (page 38). Encourage them to practice proofreading skills as they complete the worksheet.

STEP 4: EDITING

Have students check spelling, capitalization, and punctuation to allow for easier reading. Use peer editing at this step, as well as student-teacher writing conferences. You may want to designate student editors-in-chief who specialize in punctuation and capitalization to assist other students. Spelling resources can consist of the word wall, environmental print in the room, dictionaries, the Spell-It-Right reproducible (page 85), and the other students in the class. Encourage students to identify and circle their errors.
• Editing Practice
Have students edit the story on the My Trip reproducible (page 39).

STEP 5: PUBLISHING

Invite students to neatly rewrite or type their story. Have students include illustrations if appropriate. Display final products on bulletin boards, compile them into a classroom book, arrange them into a newspaper, tape them on a cassette, or have students act them out as a script, send them as a letter, or simply read them aloud.

MY BEST BIRTHDAY EVER
PREWRITING PRACTICE

Name _____ Date _____

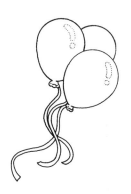

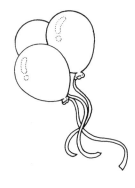

Prewriting is the first step of the writing process.
This is when you choose your topic
and you write down as many related details as
possible. Your prewriting can be a web,
a list, or a picture. These details do not have
to be in complete sentences.

Directions: Fill in the bubbles with interesting details about the topic. Add more bubbles
if you run out of room.

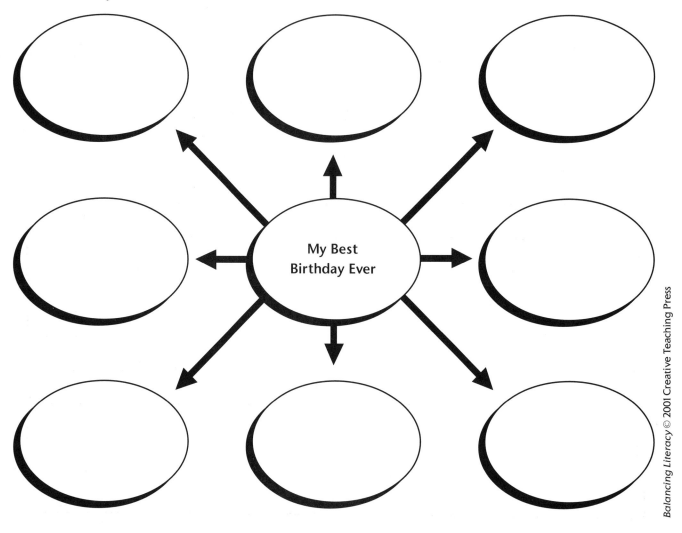

My Best
Birthday Ever

Balancing Literacy © 2001 Creative Teaching Press

MY BEST BIRTHDAY EVER
DRAFTING PRACTICE

Name _____ Date _____

> Drafting is when you take the information listed from
> your prewriting and put it into complete sentences. You can
> also add details that you may not have included in the
> prewriting stage. If you are unsure of how to spell a word, just
> write it the way it sounds for now. The most important thing
> is that you get all your ideas down on paper.

Directions: Write a story using the web you completed during prewriting. Write on the back of this
page if you need more room.

TOOTH STORY
REVISING PRACTICE

Name _____   Date _____

Directions: Read through the story below. First, underline the topic sentence. Then, add a proper ending to the story. Finally, come up with a title for the story.

_____
Title

    Last week when I went to the park with my father and sister, I thought it was going to be another ordinary day. It started out the same as usual. First, we walked by the pond and fed the ducks. Next, we got on our bikes and rode on the trails. Then, we took out a board game, and my sister won three times in a row! After that, we went on the playground to have some more fun. We were so tired from everything we did, that it was finally time to sit down on the blanket and eat some lunch.

    I was chewing my tuna fish sandwich when I noticed something hard. I spit it out to see what it was and I saw one of my teeth lying there in my hand! This had only happened to me a couple of times before so I was really excited. Most of my other friends lost all their teeth already.

_____

_____

_____

_____

_____

_____

_____

_____

_____

_____

_____

Balancing Literacy © 2001 Creative Teaching Press

MY TRIP
EDITING PRACTICE

Name _____ Date _____

I whet to Disney World with my mom an my bothir

an sistr. First I whet on a warter rid an I got wet

becase the warter spasht on me. Next we woched a

show that was really funne. then I saw Mickey Mouse

an Minney Mouse. what a great time we had Finally I

sed bye to Disney World an we whet to the hotel

Directions
1. Circle the two words that are supposed to be capitalized.
2. Find the two places where the author forgot to put a punctuation mark at the end of a sentence. Add the appropriate punctuation marks.
3. Add quotation marks "" when the writer uses dialogue in the story.
4. The word "and" is misspelled 5 times in the story. Cross out the misspelled word in the story each time and write it correctly.
5. There are 14 other misspelled words in this story. Circle all the ones you can find and try to write them correctly.

Balancing Literacy © 2001 Creative Teaching Press

WRITING DOMAINS

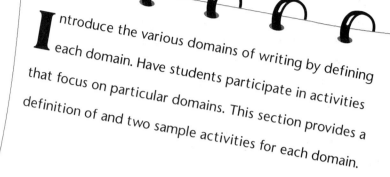

I ntroduce the various domains of writing by defining each domain. Have students participate in activities that focus on particular domains. This section provides a definition of and two sample activities for each domain.

NARRATIVE

The writer tells a story using a sequence of events and includes story elements (e.g., setting, characters). In a personal narrative, the writer tells about a situation in his or her own life.

- Have students use the sequence words listed on the Sequence Words reproducible (page 42) to write a personal narrative.

- Invite students to write a narrative paragraph about one character from a story.

DESCRIPTIVE

The writer uses description, including physical and sensory details, to help the reader see a picture.

- Have students write a poem on the My Cinquain reproducible (page 43).

- Cut out landscape pictures from magazines, and give each student one picture. Encourage students to write a descriptive paragraph about their picture. Display the pictures, and read one of the descriptive paragraphs. Invite the class to identify which picture you described.

PERSUASIVE

The writer states an opinion and tries to convince the reader to agree; the writer anticipates and addresses the reader's concerns.

- Have students create an original product (e.g., Joe's Frizzles Shampoo) and write a commercial persuading people to buy it.

- Invite students to write a persuasive letter to explain why they should have an extra recess. Go over the format for a friendly letter beforehand.

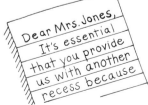

Dear Mrs. Jones,
It's essential
that you provide
us with another
recess because

EXPOSITORY (INFORMATIVE)

The writer includes an explanation with facts and information.

- Invite students to be newspaper reporters. Encourage them to find out about school events or interview school staff. Invite them to write articles based on the information they found.

- Have students make a travel brochure for a city or place. Invite students to research their topic by looking in encyclopedias or on the Internet. Have them write a historical background and list places of interest on the Travel Brochure reproducible (page 44). Encourage them to add illustrations. Have students write their name on the back of their brochure.

IMAGINATIVE

The writer creatively tells a story about a fictional situation.

- Have students write about a topic from the Imaginative Writing Topics reproducible (page 45). Place a copy of the topics in the writing center for student reference.

- Fill a box with approximately 20 unusual or interesting objects (e.g., tennis ball, feather). Have students choose an object from the box and write a story about it.

EXPRESSIVE (REFLECTIVE)

The writer puts careful thought into a topic or situation.

- Have students write in various types of journals. (See the Journal Writing section on pages 49–50.)

SEQUENCE WORDS

Name _____ Date _____

Directions: Use the sequence words listed below to write a personal narrative. Give your story a title and highlight the sequence words you used.

Title _____

First

Next

Then

After that

Finally

_____
_____
_____
_____
_____
_____
_____
_____
_____
_____
_____
_____
_____
_____
_____
_____
_____

MY CINQUAIN

Name _____   Date _____

Title (1 word)

Describes the title (2 words)

Describes an action of the title (3 words)

Describes your feeling about the title (4 words)

Renames the title (1 word)

Example:

Fog
Fluffy, thick
Blowing, rolling, covering
It makes me shiver
Clouds

TRAVEL BROCHURE

Location

Historical Background

Places of Interest

Climate _____

IMAGINATIVE WRITING TOPICS

A Day at the Circus

If I could live anywhere . . .

What if all the snow turned to ice cream?

What would you do if you lived in a television set?

If I had three wishes . . .

If money grew on trees . . .

What if it rained for 100 days straight?

Imagine if you were the only person who could fly.

If I were the teacher for a day . . .

WRITING FOLDERS

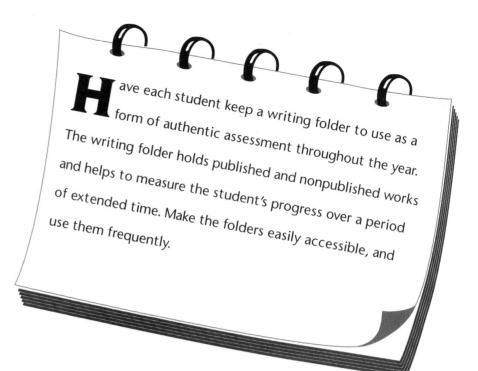

Have each student keep a writing folder to use as a form of authentic assessment throughout the year. The writing folder holds published and nonpublished works and helps to measure the student's progress over a period of extended time. Make the folders easily accessible, and use them frequently.

STUDENT RESOURCES

Have some writing resources kept at students' fingertips right inside the folders. These resources could include the Imaginative Writing Topics (page 45), Portfolio Conference Record (page 48), Spell-It-Right (page 85), and Editing Checklist (page 87) reproducibles. Keep additional copies of these resources in the writing center at all times. Encourage students to explore various writing genres. Give each student the My Writing Checklist (page 47) to keep in the writing folder. Invite students to keep track of each genre they have written by checking it off on the checklist.

WRITING CONFERENCES

Use the Portfolio Conference Record during student/teacher writing conferences. The purpose of these conferences is to review the student's work and identify strengths and areas in need of improvement. Record selected samples along with the date on the conference sheet, or have students record this information. Note the main points of

the conference and any goals for improvement. The more students are involved in this process, the greater the results will be. Keep each student's completed form in his or her portfolio.

rough drafts
forms
final drafts

AUTHOR'S CHAIR

Designate an "Author's Chair" for students who volunteer to read their stories. The Author's Chair motivates students to share their work with the rest of the class and makes students feel like "published" authors. Invite five students to comment on what they liked about the author's story.

MY WRITING CHECKLIST

Keep track of the genres you use in your writing. Place a check in the box next to each genre you have used.

Genre

Adventure								
Advertisement								
Article								
Autobiography								
Biography								
Book review								
Card								
Cartoon								
Character study								
Descriptive								
Diary/Journal								
Fable								
Folktale/Legend								
Humor								
Imaginative								
Instructions								
Invitation								
Letter								
Mystery								
Narrative								
Opinion								
Persuasive								
Play								
Poetry								
Poster								
Recipe								
Research project								
Riddles or joke								
Song								
Speech								

Name _____

PORTFOLIO CONFERENCE RECORD

Name _____

Date	Sample	Student/Teacher Comments

Balancing Literacy © 2001 Creative Teaching Press

JOURNAL WRITING

Journals give students the opportunity to think about what they have read and make connections from the text to real life. They also give students the opportunity to freely express themselves and their views and provide teachers with a way to monitor each student's literacy development. Have students use notebooks, composition books, or stapled pieces of lined paper as journals.

There are several types of journals that students can keep. The following section presents some of these types.

DIALOGUE JOURNALS

These journals emphasize meaning of text while providing natural, functional experiences both in writing and reading. An example of a dialogue journal is a Buddy Journal. Buddy Journals encourage written conversation between students using a journal format. Buddies write back and forth to each other about anything they wish.

DOUBLE-ENTRY JOURNALS

This type of journal provides students with an opportunity to identify text passages that are interesting or meaningful to them and to explain why in writing. These journals are divided into two columns. Students write quotes from the text in one column and their personal responses or reactions to the quotes in the other column.

LITERARY JOURNALS

Literary journals are where students write about text that they have read. Type a list of questions, and make copies of the list. Give each student a copy to glue onto the inside front cover of his or her literary journal. Students can refer to these questions each time they respond to a reading. Some questions to include are *Who are the main characters? Where does the story take place? What problems were presented in the story? How did you feel about the story? Why would you recommend (or not recommend) this book to a friend?*

REFLECTIVE JOURNALS

Reflective journals give students the opportunity to write about something that happened and how they feel about it. Students also include what they learned from the event.

LEARNING LOGS

These journals are used for students to respond to specific questions or to write about what they learned. These logs can be used for any area of the curriculum. Have students respond in paragraph form to a topic or question (e.g., This is everything I learned about life cycles or What is a community?). Have students record metacognitive thoughts in math journals. Students explain their thinking process while performing a problem or completing a process (e.g., How do you know what time it is when you look at a clock?). These learning logs and journals integrate other subject areas with writing skills and can help the teacher assess the student's understanding of the topic.

Spelling and Phonics

Spelling is the orthography of words, and phonics refers to the sound-symbol relationships. Spelling and phonics are interrelated processes; both involve readers and writers in using, analyzing, and decoding words. Students use phonics as a basis when writing words letter by letter or part by part as they spell them out. Conversely, students may notice phonetic patterns while practicing spelling words.

Only about half of the words in the English language are phonetically regular, so students cannot solely rely on phonics as a means of learning spelling. Students need to have a wide range of language knowledge and strategies combined with an understanding of how words look and what they mean. Word walls and exposure to high-frequency word lists offer students practice with how words look.

It is important for students to correct the spelling in their own written work. Use students' own writings when searching for spelling words. This makes learning how to spell the words more meaningful.

Integrate the spelling and phonics lessons in this section with your reading and writing instruction.

METHODS OF SPELLING INSTRUCTION

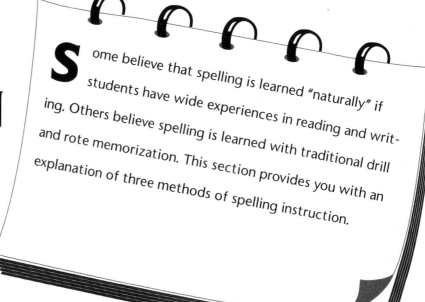

Some believe that spelling is learned "naturally" if students have wide experiences in reading and writing. Others believe spelling is learned with traditional drill and rote memorization. This section provides you with an explanation of three methods of spelling instruction.

DEVELOPMENTAL APPROACH

Learning to spell is a gradual process and is not limited to memorizing lists. English spelling has a system that can be learned, but it is not expected that a student will immediately learn the conventions of spelling. Generally, students move through five stages before becoming proficient spellers.

Stages of Spelling Development
- Precommunicative Stage
  - No sound-symbol correspondence
  - Scribbling, pictures, letters, numbers
  - Unsystematic and random strings of letters are used to carry meaning
  - Nonreaders
- Semiphonetic Stage
  - Some sound-symbol correspondence
  - Use of one or two letters to represent a word (e.g., c = see, y = why)
  - May not have concept of what a word is
- Phonetic Stage
  - Uses letters to represent phonemes; spelling by sound

- Represents the entire sound structure of a word (e.g., stopt = stopped)
- Transitional Stage
  - Spells by the way the word looks
  - Internalizes information about spelling patterns (e.g., whith = with)
  - Conventions and rules (doubling consonants, vowel combinations) aren't mastered
- Conventional Stage
  - Most words are spelled correctly
  - Developed over time (approximately by fourth grade)

PATTERN APPROACH

In this method, the teacher introduces words and patterns. Begin with a list of words, and focus on the general principle(s) represented by the words in the list (e.g., short *a*, *cat*, *mat*, and *apple*). Students practice words by hearing, seeing, and writing them. The purpose of learning to spell is to use the words correctly in writing. Students use the words in a meaningful way (e.g., writing letters to someone). They look over their writing and check for any misspelled words. Once the class understands a spelling pattern, reinforce and extend it by brainstorming other words that fit the pattern. (See the word lists on pages 62–63.)

INTEGRATED APPROACH

In an integrated spelling program, students discover and apply the rules and patterns. Students have directed daily practice and participate in spelling center activities. A proofreading system indicating that learners know that temporary inventive spellings are being used to get meaning down during initial composition is also used.

Post word lists in the room to show expectations for correct spelling every time the learner writes. Encourage students to use a variety of resources, including a dictionary, a word wall, peers, and charts. Assess students with rubrics, checklists, and mini-conferences.

WORD CHUNKS

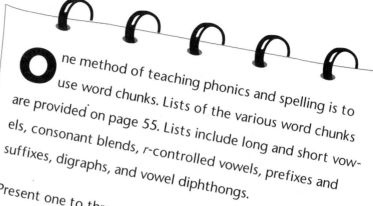

One method of teaching phonics and spelling is to use word chunks. Lists of the various word chunks are provided on page 55. Lists include long and short vowels, consonant blends, r-controlled vowels, prefixes and suffixes, digraphs, and vowel diphthongs.

Present one to three word chunks to the class weekly. The number of chunks will vary depending upon the students' readiness to learn the concepts. Post a list of these word chunks in an area of the classroom after they are introduced so students can refer to the list when necessary.

VOWEL CHUNK BOOKS

Make several copies of the Vowel Chunks reproducible (page 56), and give one to each student. Choose a vowel (e.g., *a*), and have students write the vowel in the tree trunks. Have students write the vowel chunks (e.g., short *a—ap, at*, or long *a—ate, age*) in the crown of the trees. Have students look through magazines or books for words that

have any of the vowel chunks in them (e.g., *map, sat, mate, cage*) and record them on their reproducible page. Choose a different vowel, and have students repeat the activity. Have students compile their completed pages to make a "Vowel Chunk" book.

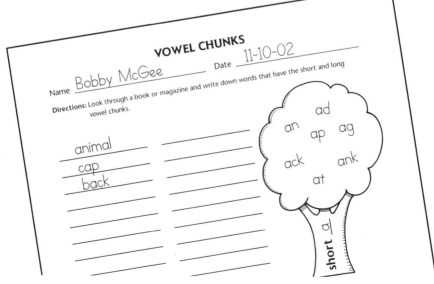

WORD CHUNK LIST

Short Vowels

ab	ad	ag	al	am	an	ap	at	ax	ack	ank	ash
ed	eg	em	en	et	ell	est					
id	ig	im	in	ip	it	ix	ick	ill	ing	ink	
ob	od	og	om	on	op	ot	ox	ock			
ub	ud	ug	um	un	up	us	ut	uck	ump	unk	

Long Vowels

ai	ay	ace	ail	ain	ake	ame	ate			
ea	ee									
igh	ie	ide	ike	ine	ite					
oa	oe	ow	oat	ode	oke	old	one	ose	ote	
ue	use	ute								

Consonant Blends

bl	br	cl	cr	dr	fl	fr	gl	gr	pl	pr	sc
scr	shr	sk	sl	sm	sn	sp	spl	spr	squ	st	str
sw	thr	tr	tw								

Endings

ck	ct	ft	ld	le	lf	lk	lm	lp	lt	mp	nd
ng	nk	nt	pt	rd	rk	rl	rm	rn	rt	sk	sp
st	nch	tch									

Digraphs

ch	gh	ph	qu	sh	th	wh

R-Controlled Vowels ("Bossy R")

ar	er	ir	or	ur

Vowel Diphthongs

au	aw	ew	ey	ion	oi	ou	oy	ui	uy	oo	ow
ai	ea	ere	are								

Prefixes

bi-	co-	de-	dis-	ex-	im-	in-	mid-	mis-	non-	pre-	re-
sub-	un-										

Suffixes

-able	-ed	-en	-er	-est	-ful	-ing	-ish	-less	-ly	-ment	-ness
-ship	-ward										

VOWEL CHUNKS

Name _____   Date _____

Directions: Look through a book or magazine and write down words that have the short and long vowel chunks.

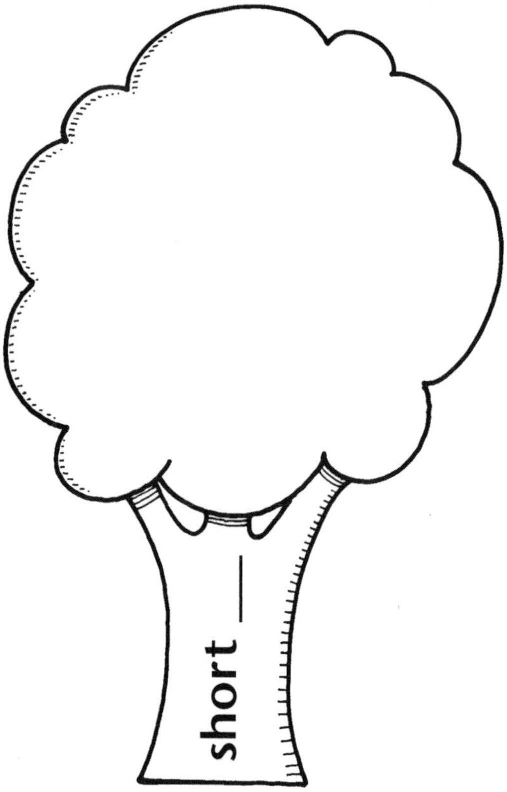

_____   _____

_____   _____

_____   _____

_____   _____

_____   _____

_____   _____

_____   _____

short

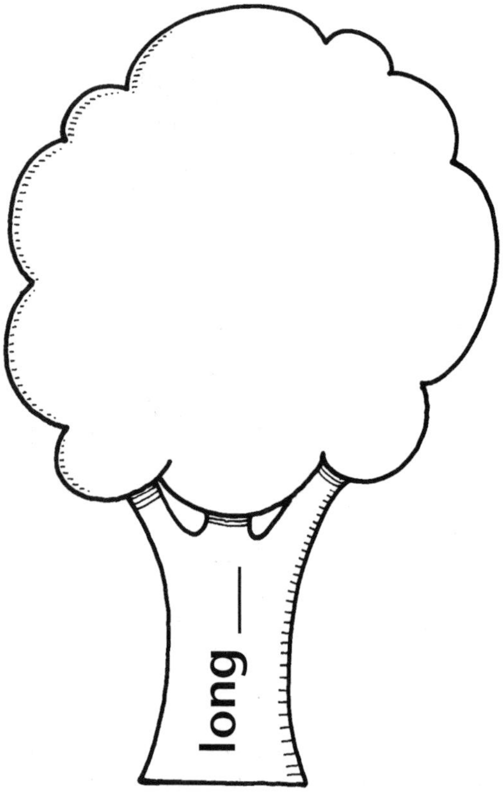

long

_____   _____

_____   _____

_____   _____

_____   _____

_____   _____

_____   _____

_____   _____

_____   _____

WORD WALLS

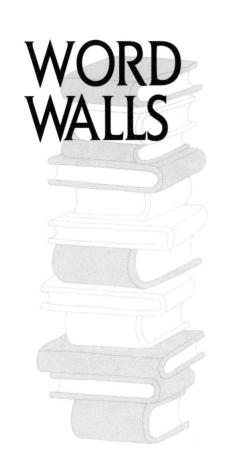

A word wall is a valuable resource for students when writing. It is an organized collection of words displayed on a classroom wall. Word walls should be visible and accessible to all students in the classroom. Start out small and grow as the year progresses, never exceeding 120 words at one time. It is helpful for the students to have the words on different-colored backgrounds to assist in locating them. You may want to color-code words by pattern or spelling principle. Teach students to use the word wall on a daily basis, and include it in weekly whole-group activities as well.

It is important that the students become very familiar with the words and that the words have real meaning to them. Include weekly spelling words and words of the week. Choose the words students will use the most.

Use a word wall to
- support the teaching of important general principles about words and how they work
- foster reading and writing
- provide reference support for students during reading and writing
- promote independence as students work with words
- provide a visual to help students remember connections between words and the characteristics that will help them form categories

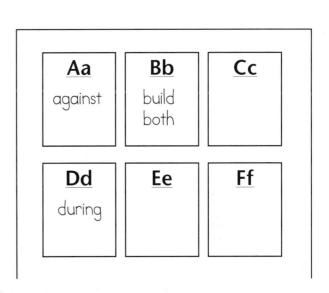

CHOOSE WORDS

When choosing words for your word wall, select words that

- are high frequency.
- students use in their group or independent writing.
- students have difficulty writing.
- students request often to be spelled.
- serve as examples of spelling patterns (e.g., letter clusters, vowel combinations, prefixes, or contractions). See pages 62–63 for a list of words categorized by spelling patterns.

UPDATE WORDS

A word wall is a continual work in progress. Update it according to the following guidelines:

- Add and remove words depending on your teaching needs.
- Add a word by calling attention to and reviewing its spelling and definition.
- Remove words that are no longer needed.

HIGH-FREQUENCY WORDS

The words that appear in printed materials most often are referred to as high-frequency words. Some high-frequency words are phonetic, such as *am, man,* and *moon,* and some can be learned through picture clues, such as *mother, number,* and *rain.* However, many of them do not follow standard phonetic principles and all are encountered so frequently that recognizing them by sight improves reading fluency. Students learn the spelling of these words through constant exposure to them. Refer to the list of high-frequency words on pages 60–61.

PERSONAL WORD WALLS

Have students keep a personal word wall in their writing folders. Give each student three copies of the Personal Word Wall Reproducible (page 64). Have students label each box with a letter, beginning with *Aa* and ending with *Zz.* Have students write some of the words from the class word wall on their personal word wall. Encourage students to add words to their personal word wall and refer to them as necessary when writing.

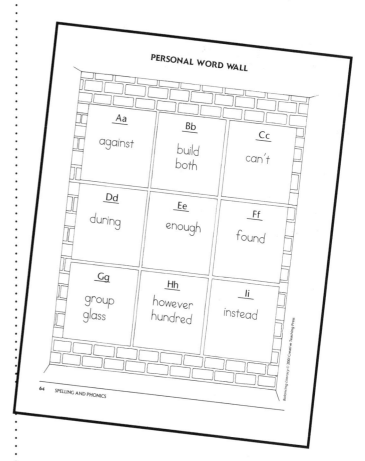

Word Wall Activities

Use the following activities to introduce and give students practice with the words on your word wall.

INTRODUCE A NEW WORD

Have students look at and say the word. Have them write it in their personal word wall. If needed, invite students to look up the word in a dictionary. Ask volunteers to use the word in a sentence.

MYSTERY WORD

Pick a word from the word wall to be the "mystery word." Give students clues about the word, and have them guess what it is. For example, if the mystery word is *chores* you might say *It is a noun, there are two vowels in the word, and it begins with a consonant blend.* If students do not correctly identify the word, give them more clues until they are able to identify it.

BUILDING A WORD WALL SENTENCE

When you have several words up on your word wall, have students make sentences using only the words on the word wall and proper names.

HANGMAN

Choose a word from the word wall. Draw a blank line for each letter of the word on the chalkboard. Invite students to take turns guessing the letters in the word. If a student guesses a correct letter, place that letter on the corresponding blank line. If a student guesses an incorrect letter, write that letter in a box. Have students continue to guess letters until they are able to identify the word.

HIGH-FREQUENCY WORD LIST

able	boat	draw	go
above	body	dry	going
across	book	during	gold
add	both	early	gone
again	bottom	earth	good
against	box	easy	got
ago	boy	eat	great
air	bring	either	green
almost	brought	else	ground
alone	build	end	group
already	built	English	grow
also	came	enough	half
although	cannot	even	hand
always	can't	ever	happened
am	car	every	hard
American	care	everyone	head
among	carefully	everything	hear
animal	carry	example	heard
another	center	face	heart
answer	certain	fact	heavy
any	change	fall	held
anything	check	family	help
area	children	far	here
around	city	fast	high
asked	class	father	him
away	close	feel	himself
back	cold	feet	his
ball	come	felt	hold
beautiful	common	few	home
became	complete	follow	horse
because	country	food	hot
become	course	foot	hour
before	cut	form	house
began	dark	found	however
begin	day	four	hundred
behind	deep	friend	ice
being	didn't	front	idea
below	different	full	I'll
best	distance	game	I'm
better	does	gave	important
between	dog	get	inside
big	done	girl	instead
black	don't	give	itself
blue	door	glass	job

HIGH-FREQUENCY WORD LIST

just	new	rock	surface
keep	next	room	system
kept	night	round	table
kind	nothing	run	take
knew	notice	sad	talk
land	number	same	tall
language	off	sat	tell
large	often	saw	ten
last	oh	say	that's
later	old	school	themselves
lay	once	sea	thing
learn	open	second	think
learned	order	seen	third
least	other	sentence	those
leave	our	set	though
leaves	outside	several	thought
left	own	shall	three
less	page	ship	through
let	paper	short	tiny
letter	part	should	to
life	past	show	today
light	pattern	shown	together
line	perhaps	side	told
list	person	simple	too
live	picture	since	took
lived	piece	six	top
living	place	size	toward
longer	plants	sky	town
look	play	small	tree
low	point	snow	true
main	poor	someone	turn
man	possible	something	turned
map	power	soon	under
matter	probably	sound	understand
me	problem	space	United States
mean	put	special	until
men	question	stand	upon
might	quite	start	us
mind	rain	state	usually
miss	ran	stay	voice
money	read	still	walked
moon	reading	stood	want
morning	ready	stop	warm
mother	real	story	watch
move	really	strong	yes
much	red	study	yet
must	remember	such	young
name	rest	suddenly	
near	right	summer	
need	river	sun	
never	road	sure	

WORD LISTS

short *a*	short *e*	short *i*	short *o*	short *u*
apple	everyone	interest	strong	under
animal	explain	invent	clock	uncle
after	enter	dinner	beyond	unless
snacks	dressed	insect		understand
class	pencil			

long *a*	long *e*	long *i*	long *o*	long *u*
disobey	teacher	tonight	grown	chewing
entertainment	speaker	bright	borrowed	screwdriver
explain	leave	delight	unknown	newspaper
gray	breeze	frightened	following	knew
mailman	between	excitement	shoulder	threw
painting	believe		dough	through
player			though	regroup
ray			coastline	argument
remaining			throat	confuse
waist			soaking	truth
yesterday			thorough	congratulations

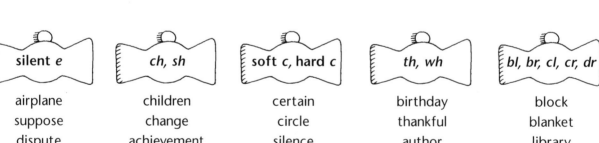

silent *e*	ch, sh	soft *c*, hard *c*	th, wh	bl, br, cl, cr, dr
airplane	children	certain	birthday	block
suppose	change	circle	thankful	blanket
dispute	achievement	silence	author	library
gate	reach	decide	another	breakfast
alive	teacher	entrance	thousand	bridge
upside	inches	country	together	closet
true	shower	crayon	while	clothing
complete	ashamed	welcome	whisper	crown
stripe	seashore	traffic	anywhere	cradle
illustrate	pushed	cousin	whichever	drawer
	shivering	comparison	worthwhile	drinking

WORD LISTS

contractions	hard *g*, soft *g*	*fl, fr, gl, gr*	*oi, oy*	compound words
doesn't	grandfather	flavor	avoid	textbook
you're	goat	flight	moisten	football
would've	gallon	fraction	poison	everybody
we'll	garden	freedom	voice	afternoon
I'm	grateful	freeze	boiling	toothbrush
won't	giraffe	glance	rejoice	mailbox
shouldn't	general	gloves	destroy	raincoat
there's	gentle	ground	royalty	suitcase
aren't	giant	graphing	enjoyment	doorway
let's	genuine	grades	loyal	homesick
	generosity		annoyance	extraordinary

y as a vowel	double consonants	prefixes	suffixes	*y* to *ies*
suddenly	dollar	unwilling	happiness	babies
heavy	little	unknown	neatness	pennies
fearfully	tomorrow	disappear	colorful	hobbies
nursery	clapping	incorrect	hopeful	families
pretty	bottom	rebuild	wonderful	stories
buyer	mattress	rewrite	beautiful	fairies
myself	stubborn	redecorate	careless	dictionaries
dryness	arrange	prevent	agreement	
crying	effort	prepaid	loveable	
flyer	winner	midnight	noticeable	
technology	possibility	disappointment	greenish	

-tch	*qu, ph*	silent *kn, wr, gh*	*oo*	*ow, ou*
scratch	question	knife	moonlight	drowsy
patch	quarter	knees	balloon	crowded
matching	quiet	knock	afternoon	powerful
catcher	quarrel	knowledge	loose	allowance
batch	quality	wrong	bedroom	frown
fetch	earthquake	wrapper	bookmark	fountain
	phrase	wrinkle	looking	shout
	alphabet	wrist	stood	mouthful
	telephone	wrestling	crooked	round
	photograph	enough	cookie	lousy
	phonics	laughter	neighborhood	outstanding

PERSONAL WORD WALL

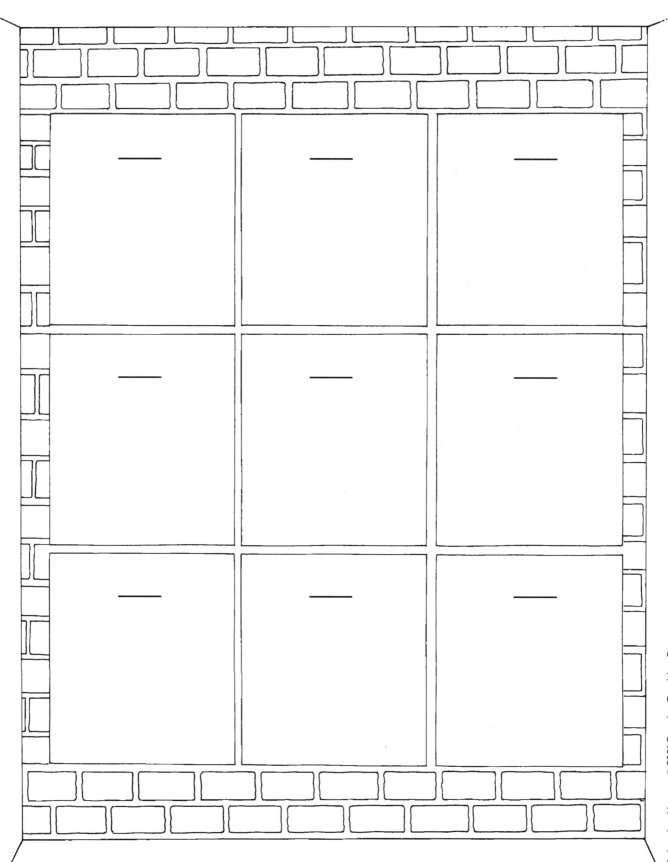

SPELLING ACTIVITIES AND GAMES

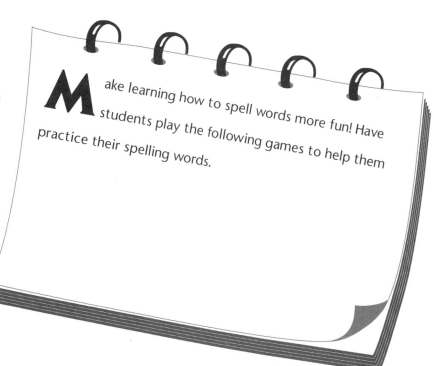

Make learning how to spell words more fun! Have students play the following games to help them practice their spelling words.

DICTIONARY GAME

Divide the class into pairs. Give each pair a dictionary. Write a spelling word on the chalkboard. Invite pairs to work together to look for the word in the dictionary and raise their hands when they find it. Give the first three pairs to raise their hands a sticker. Have a volunteer tell which page number the definition is on so everyone can turn to that page and read the definition together. Give all players a sticker at the end of the game for their hard work. Invite students to place their sticker next to the word on their personal word wall (page 64).

MISSING LETTERS

Write the spelling words on the chalkboard but draw lines in place of two or three letters of each word (e.g., b_ca_se). Challenge volunteers to fill in the blanks to complete each spelling word. Invite the class to spell out the words together.

GROUP CHEER

Choose one student as the leader of the cheer. For extra fun, give him or her a pom-pom to use to motivate the rest of the class. Have the student lead the class in chanting each letter of a spelling word. For example, the leader says *Give me a* c and the class repeats the letter. Then, have the leader say *What does that spell?* Encourage the class to respond with the word.

VOCABULARY VOLLEYBALL

Draw a volleyball court on a large piece of tagboard, and place a piece of Velcro on each side of the court. Make a cardboard volleyball, and place a piece of Velcro on the back of it. Display the court so the entire class can see it. Divide the class into two teams. Have one team sit in a line to the left of you and the other sit in a line to the right of you. Place the volleyball on the left side of the court. This represents that it is the turn of the team to the left of you. Ask that team *Which word means the same as "really good"?* Invite the first person in line for that team to answer the question. If he or she is correct, the ball is hit over the "net" to the other side. If he or she answers incorrectly, the other team gets a point and the "ball." The opposing team gets a new question and if their team member answers it correctly, the ball goes back to the other side. Continue in this manner until a team gets 10 points.

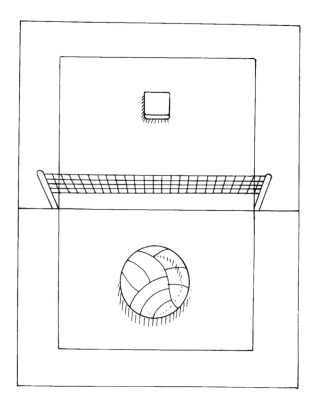

JEOPARDY

Make a Jeopardy board by gluing 16 library card pockets on a piece of poster board. Arrange the pockets so there are four rows and four columns. Number the pockets in each row as follows: 1st–10, 2nd–20, 3rd–30, 4th–40. The number refers to the difficulty of the question (10 being the least difficult and 40 being the most difficult). Label each column with a category (e.g., spelling, definitions, syllables, synonyms). Write four questions for each category (e.g., How do you spell *caterpillar*? What is the definition of *enormous*? How many syllables are there in the word *extraordinary*? Name a synonym for *little*.). Write each question on a separate index card. Place one card in each corresponding pocket of the chart. Place easier questions in the 10 and 20 pockets and more challenging questions in the 30 and 40 pockets. Divide the class into two teams, and seat them on separate sides of the classroom. Display the board so both teams can see it. Invite one player on Team A to choose a number (10, 20, 30, or 40) and a category. Read the card, and encourage player 1 to answer the question or complete the task. If he or she answers correctly, the team gets the appropriate number of points. If he or she answers incorrectly, Team B gets a chance to answer. If Team B answers correctly, they receive the points. Continue in the same manner, alternating turns between each team until every card has been chosen. The team with the most points wins.

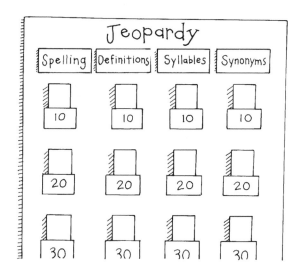

SPELLING TIC-TAC-TOE

Divide the class into two teams (*X*'s and *O*'s). Draw a large tic-tac-toe board on the chalkboard. Say a spelling word, and invite the first student on the X team to spell the word. If the student spells the word correctly, his or her team gets to place an X on the tic-tac-toe board. If he or she spells the word incorrectly, it's the other team's turn. Continue in this manner until one team gets tic-tac-toe. Play several rounds to be sure all class members get a chance to participate and all the spelling words are used.

GUESS THE WORD

Choose several spelling words. Write sentences on sentence strips, but leave a blank where a spelling word would fit in. Read aloud the sentences, one at a time, with the class, and have volunteers fill in the missing words. Then, reread the completed sentences with the whole class.

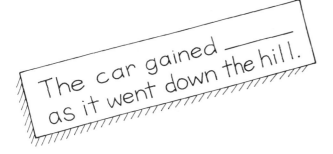

The car gained _____ as it went down the hill.

WORD SEARCH

Have students practice writing and locating their spelling words by having them complete a Partner Word Search (page 68). Invite students to write the spelling words in the grid by placing one letter in each square. Words can be arranged vertically, horizontally, or diagonally. Have students "hide" their words by placing a random letter in each empty square. Encourage students to write the words that they hid in the Word Bank box so their partner will know which words to look for. Have students trade papers and complete their partner's word search.

VOWEL DIPHTHONGS

Give each student a Vowel Diphthongs reproducible (page 69). Have students combine consonants with vowel diphthongs to make words. Have students write their words on the blank lines. Invite students to complete this worksheet as an independent activity, or turn the activity into a game by setting a time limit and having students compete to see who can make the most words in two minutes.

PARTNER WORD SEARCH

Name _____   Date _____

Directions: Using the assigned word list, hide the words in a word search for a classmate. When you are done, exchange papers and complete your partner's word search.

Word Bank

Partner's Name _____

VOWEL DIPHTHONGS

Name _____ Date _____

<table>
<tr><td align="center">Group A</td><td align="center">Group B</td></tr>
</table>

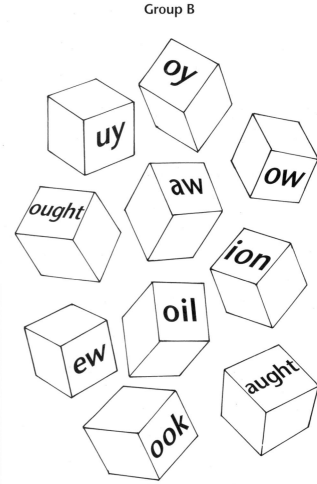

How many words can you make by combining two of the blocks together, one from each group?

_____ _____ _____

_____ _____ _____

_____ _____ _____

_____ _____ _____

_____ _____ _____

_____ _____ _____

_____ _____ _____

Balancing Your Literacy Program

Now that you have an understanding of the various components of a balanced literacy program and ideas for activities and lessons, you may be asking how do I implement all these things into my classroom schedule? Unfortunately, there isn't one approach that applies to everyone. The approach you select will depend on your daily time frame as well as your school's requirements and curriculum. Combine activities presented in the Reading, Writing, and Spelling and Phonics sections to create a literacy program, or choose a teaching method that incorporates several components and build your program around it.

This section presents three different methods of integrating several components. Reader's and Writer's Workshop, Literature Circles, and Literacy Centers each provide ways to include several components while allowing students to work independently on various literacy tasks. This frees you to work with small groups on guided reading, mini-lessons, or any other literacy skill.

Remember, regardless of which approach you decide to implement, time is required to introduce students to the procedures and process. Do not expect to introduce a method and have it running smoothly in your class within a week. The time spent on the initial stages is well worth it in the end. Making sure students understand the entire process and procedures will result in an efficient and effective literacy program.

CLASSROOM ENVIRONMENT

How should your classroom be set up and what are some of the materials you should have available for student use? This section provides you with a diagram suggesting how you can set up your room (see page 72) and the following list to help you answer these questions.

When you walk into a balanced literacy classroom you may see any of the following:
- a large area for demonstrations and meetings that will develop a sense of community
- areas for small-group, partner, and independent work
- quiet areas separated from noisy areas
- a classroom library with an abundance of books for independent and instructional reading
- reading materials, including children's literature, predictable books, trade books, newspapers, student-made books, content-related books, and magazines
- labels and directions posted
- materials easily available for student use
- stories, messages, lists, and other written materials produced by students through interactive writing
- students involved in activities to increase comprehension
- computer(s) and educational software
- reference materials—dictionaries, thesaurus, word wall
- published versions of students' independent writing for others to read
- ongoing informal and formal assessment used to monitor student progress
- the teacher modifying instruction based on students' needs
- student discussions, teacher-student conferences
- the teacher using a variety of methods and materials to teach reading and writing
- students working in whole-group, small-group, paired, and individual settings
- portfolios and authentic assessment

SETTING UP YOUR CLASSROOM

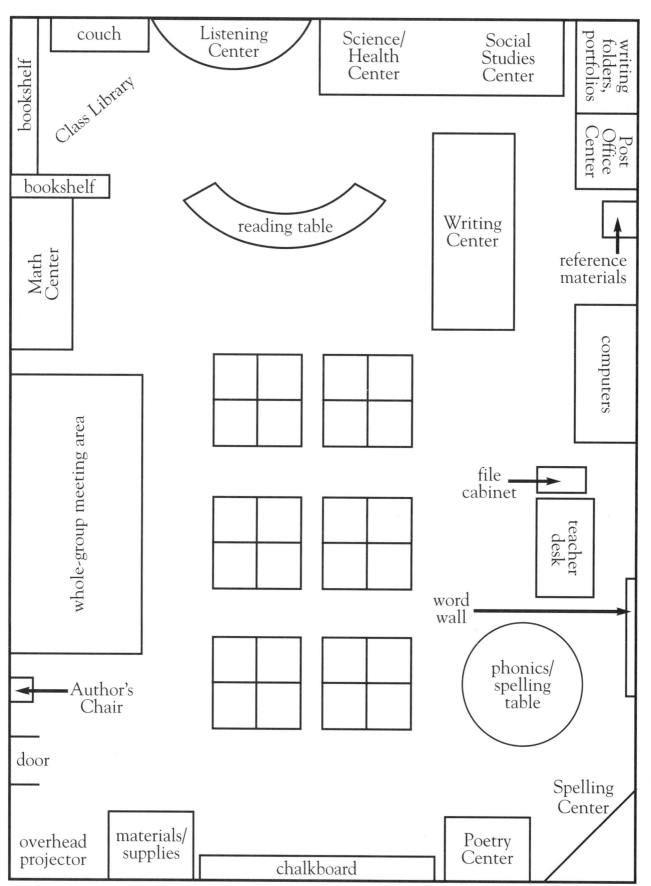

READER'S WORKSHOP

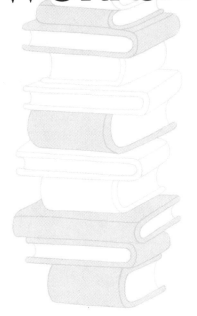

Reader's Workshop is a method of teaching reading and vocabulary skills that allows students a choice in what they read and provides time for independent reading. Research has shown that students who have a hand in choosing what they read will have a greater sense of involvement and have more of an investment in the work they do. Reader's Workshop also allows you to set individual goals and expectations for each student based on his or her strengths and needs. Generally, the workshop begins with a mini-lesson that focuses on a reading skill or concept. Then, students are encouraged to read independently for approximately 20 minutes (S.S.R. or buddy reading with a partner). Students respond by writing in a reading journal or by writing letters to the teacher. Students can respond about the content, genre, or author's style or give a book review. At the end of the workshop, students talk to each other about the books they have read. To ensure that students are on-task and held accountable for their reading, have them record the titles of text read on their reading log (page 22).

MINI-LESSONS

Use mini-lessons to focus on a wide variety of reading skills and concepts. Work for five to ten minutes with either a small group or the whole class. Suggested topics include the following:

Reading strategies
Drawing conclusions
Main idea
Sequence
Recalling details
Context clues
Making inferences
Critical thinking skills
Word meaning strategies
Cause/Effect
Making analogies

Fact and opinion
Classifying
Following directions
Listening skills
Speaking skills
Dictionary skills
Library/Research skills

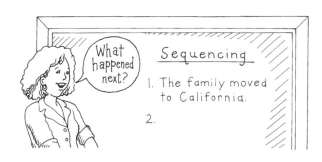

Reader's Workshop Schedule

The time you schedule for each stage of the workshop will depend on the needs of your students. Adapt the schedule shown below to work with your daily classroom routine and curriculum goals.

Mini-lesson (5–10 minutes)

Independent Reading (10–20 minutes)
Have students read independently.

Workshop (20–40 minutes)
Have students do any of the following activities during this time. Have students respond about what they read by writing in a literary journal (page 50), writing letters, or completing a Book Review reproducible (page 75). Invite small groups of students to read the same text and hold group meetings to discuss the text read. Conduct teacher-student conferences to evaluate each student's reading progress.

Sharing (5–10 minutes)
Invite students to share insights from their reading, pose questions, or share responses.

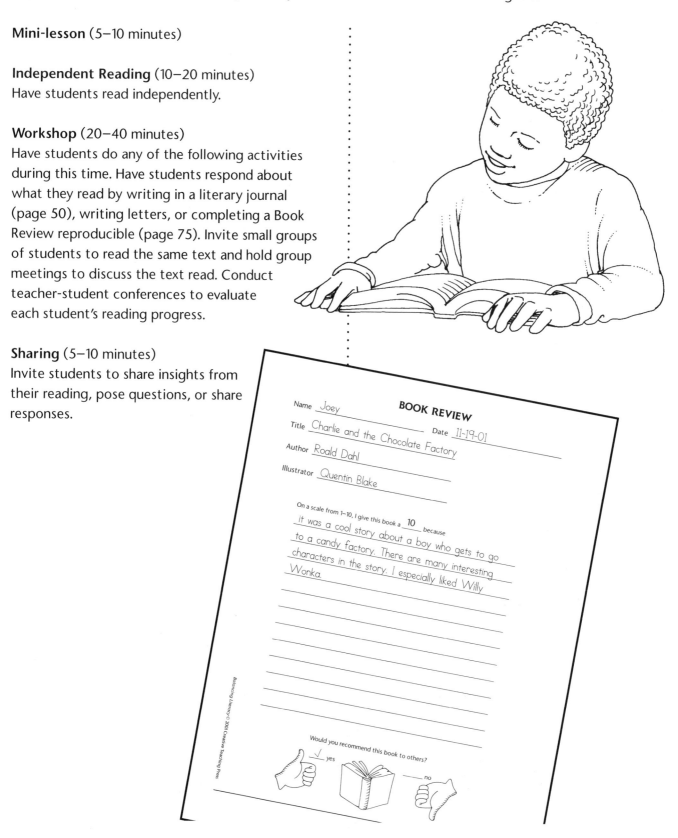

Name _Joey_

BOOK REVIEW

Title _Charlie and the Chocolate Factory_   Date _11-19-01_

Author _Roald Dahl_

Illustrator _Quentin Blake_

On a scale from 1–10, I give this book a _10_ because _it was a cool story about a boy who gets to go to a candy factory. There are many interesting characters in the story. I especially liked Willy Wonka._

Would you recommend this book to others?

✓ yes   no

BOOK REVIEW

Name _____   Date _____

Title _____

Author _____

Illustrator _____

On a scale from 1–10, I give this book a _____ because

_____

_____

_____

_____

_____

_____

_____

_____

_____

_____

_____

_____

Would you recommend this book to others?

_____ yes   _____ no

WRITER'S WORKSHOP

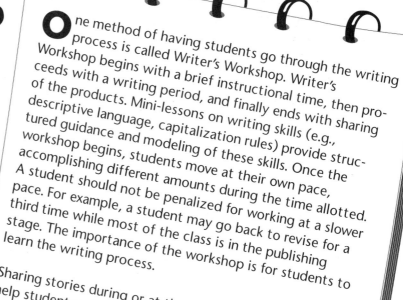

One method of having students go through the writing process is called Writer's Workshop. Writer's Workshop begins with a brief instructional time, then proceeds with a writing period, and finally ends with sharing of the products. Mini-lessons on writing skills (e.g., descriptive language, capitalization rules) provide structured guidance and modeling of these skills. Once the workshop begins, students move at their own pace, accomplishing different amounts during the time allotted. A student should not be penalized for working at a slower pace. For example, a student may go back to revise for a third time while most of the class is in the publishing stage. The importance of the workshop is for students to learn the writing process.

Sharing stories during or at the end of the workshop will help students with their listening and speaking skills, as well as help them become more developed writers. Properly demonstrate constructive criticism so students do not hurt one another's feelings. Inviting students to give feedback on each other's work allows them to become more aware of what to include and not to include in their own papers. When students realize they are writing for a purpose and know that others will see or hear their work, they tend to maximize their efforts.

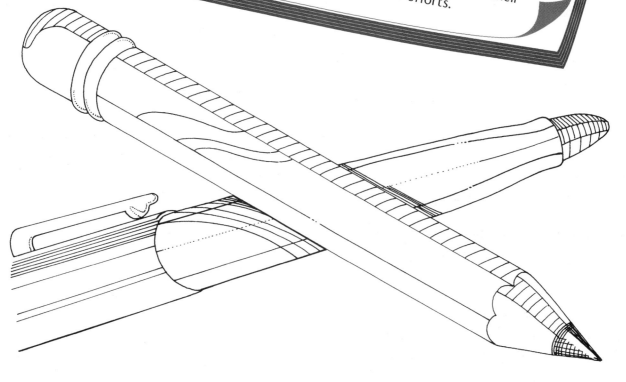

Organizing Your Materials

Place writing materials and tools in a specific area. Model proper procedures for using and storing all materials. Include a supply of paper (lined and unlined), a variety of publishing materials (e.g., scissors, hole punch, yarn, cardboard, letter stencils), a library of books from various genres, and easily accessible editing materials and reference books (e.g., dictionary, thesaurus). Be sure to designate a place for students to store their completed writing products (e.g., writing folder, portfolio).

Suggested Schedule

The time you schedule for each stage of the workshop will depend on the needs of your students. Adapt the schedule shown below to work with your daily classroom routine and curriculum goals.

Instructional Time (10 minutes)
Share teacher and student writing or conduct a mini-lesson.

Survey of Writing Plans (5 minutes)
Ask each student what his or her writing plan is for the day. Write the student's responses on the Daily Writing Plan reproducible (page 84).

Writing Time and Conferencing (25–40 minutes)
Have students write following the steps in the writing process. Conduct student conferences as needed.

Sharing (5–10 minutes)
Invite students to share their ideas, stories, and illustrations. This can be done as a whole group, with partners, or in a student-teacher conference.

MINI-LESSON TOPICS

Use mini-lessons to focus on the wide variety of writing skills and concepts. Work for five to ten minutes on a topic with either a small group or the whole class. Suggested topics include the following:

Writer's Workshop rules
Capitalization
Heading a paper
Punctuation (? . ! , "")
Letter writing format
Statements vs. questions
Handwriting and word spacing
Contractions
Writing conferences

Possessives
Antonyms
Journal writing
Synonyms
Using a writing folder
Homonyms
Using the word wall
Using the Spell-It-Right reproducible (page 85)
Homophones (hear, here)
Using personal dictionaries
Types of writing styles
Parts of speech
Good writing skills (e.g., adding details, using descriptive language)
Editing skills

Introducing Writing Stages

The following is an example of how you can introduce Writer's Workshop to your class. Introduce one stage per day, but be attentive to the needs of your class. If they need to spend more time on a particular stage, do so. It is important for the class to understand each stage in order to run effective and productive workshop periods throughout the school year.

BRAINSTORMING A TOPIC

Model how to find a topic that matters. Have students brainstorm a list of topics. Write a few of the topics on the board. Model how to leave room in between each idea. In those spaces, write down aspects of each topic. Focus on one main idea. Have students repeat the steps to write their own topics. Another way to generate topics is to have a Brainstorming Board. Hang a large piece of butcher paper on the classroom wall. Write some writing ideas on it. Leave it up for students to write any ideas they have during the school day. Have students refer to it when they need ideas for writing.

DRAFTING

Have students refer to their topics from the brainstorming session. Invite them to choose one topic to use to write a first draft. Have students circle a word when they are not sure how to spell it. Encourage them to write quickly and get down ideas rather than look up words in a dictionary. Choose three to four volunteers to read aloud their drafts. Have students put their paper in their writing folder. Review the folders before the next day's workshop.

RESPONDING AND REVISING

Have some students write while others participate in group conferences. Use group conferences to help students improve their stories. Have conference members review each other's writing and comment on it. Students may also look at published writings to get examples of how to improve their own writing (e.g., interesting introduction, use of dialogue).

IMPROVING WRITING

Demonstrate how to focus on finding an ending and an appropriate title for a story. Ask each student what his or her writing plan is for the day. Write down his or her response on the Daily Writing Plan reproducible (page 84). Encourage students to continue to write.

EDITING

Demonstrate how to determine when students are ready to edit their writing. Encourage students to ask themselves the following questions:

- Did I read the writing to myself to see if it made sense?
- Is my writing focused on one topic?
- Does my writing include details?
- Does the title fit my story?
- Did I read my story to someone else to see if it made sense?

Write these questions on a chart for student reference. Tell the class that if they answer "yes" to all the questions, they are ready to edit.

DAILY WRITING PLAN

Student	Date 11/01	Date	Date
Kelsy	1st draft My Party		
Cameron	Final Cars, Cars		
Kelly	1st draft Splat!		

During the editing stage, have students use the Spell-It-Right reproducible (page 85) to attempt to correct their spelling errors. Model the procedure to the class beforehand. Display an overhead transparency of a sample piece of writing and a Spell-It-Right reproducible. Choose a student's first draft, and use it to model how to look for misspelled words. (The student circled misspelled words during the draft stage.) Write one of the circled words in the *1st try* box. Model how to try to spell the word by sounding it out. Write that spelling in the *2nd try* box. Write another spelling in the *3rd try* box. Tell students that this is the procedure they will follow to complete a Spell-It-Right form. Demonstrate how you will correct the forms and write the correct spelling in the *Spelling* box.

Have students brainstorm a list of things to look for when editing (e.g., capital letters, punctuation, and spelling). Give each student the Editing Marks reproducible (page 86). Review each mark and what it stands for. Give each student the Editing Checklist (page 87). Read aloud and give an example of each step. Encourage students to complete a checklist each time they edit a piece of writing. Have students attach the sheet to their work and put it in a box labeled *Ready to Be Proofed*. Review the work before the next day's workshop.

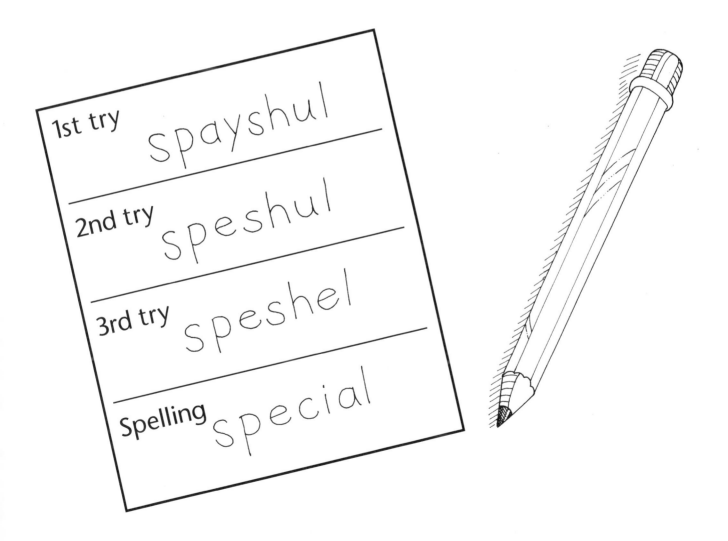

PUBLISHING

Invite students to publish their writing in any of the following ways:

- Cassette tapes—Have students tape-record their stories. Place the written story and cassette tape in a resealable plastic bag. Store the bag in the listening center. The recorded cassette tape also serves as an assessment tool for evaluating writing and speaking skills.

- Individual books—Have students bind sheets of paper together to make a book. Invite them to illustrate each page of their book as well as produce an enticing cover. Store the books in the class library for others to read.

- Dramatic script—Encourage students to create a play or dramatic skit. Have them make props and rehearse their lines. Invite students to perform in front of the rest of the class.

- Read-aloud—Invite students to sit in the Author's Chair (see page 46) and read aloud their story to the rest of the class.

- Bulletin boards—Display finished stories on a decorated bulletin board.

READER'S REVIEW

Encourage students to have their classmates read their written works. Model how to make appropriate comments, and discuss constructive criticism and positive feedback. Have students attach a Reader's Review reproducible (page 88) to their published work and place it in a designated box. Invite students to read the work and write their comments on the attached form.

READER'S AND WRITER'S WORKSHOP SCHEDULE

Arranging your schedule will depend on many factors. The following schedule suggests one possible way to incorporate Reader's and Writer's Workshop.

8:45–9:00	MORNING BUSINESS, JOURNAL WRITING
9:00–9:20	MINI-LESSON
9:20–10:20	READER'S/WRITER'S WORKSHOP
10:20–10:35	RECESS
10:35–10:50	SHARING—AUTHOR'S CHAIR
10:50–11:20	SPELLING/WORD WALL
11:20–12:00	MATH
12:00–12:45	LUNCH
12:45–1:00	SUSTAINED SILENT READING
1:00–2:00	SOCIAL STUDIES/SCIENCE
2:00–2:30	PHYSICAL EDUCATION
2:30–2:45	TEACHER READ-ALOUD
2:45–3:00	CLASS NEWS, CLEANUP

How the schedule incorporates the literacy components

Provided below is an outline of how the literacy components are included in the above schedule. Mini-lessons can cover a variety of topics, so one day a lesson may include shared reading, and another day it might be interactive writing. The workshop approach allows for the integration of several literacy components.

LITERACY COMPONENT	ACTIVITY
Modeled Reading	teacher read-aloud
Shared Reading	mini-lesson
Guided Reading	meet with small groups during "workshop" time
Independent Reading	Sustained Silent Reading
Interactive Writing	Class News (have students do some of the writing)
Modeled or Shared Writing	mini-lesson
Guided Writing	mini-lesson
Independent Writing	Writer's Workshop, journal writing

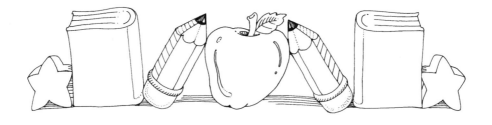

DAILY WRITING PLAN

Student	Date	Date	Date

Balancing Literacy © 2001 Creative Teaching Press

SPELL-IT-RIGHT

Name _____ Date _____

Directions: Use this sheet if you are having difficulty spelling a word and have tried other possibilities (e.g., word wall, dictionary). Make three attempts at spelling the word yourself and then have your teacher check the sheet to put the correct spelling in the final box.

1st try _____ 2nd try _____ 3rd try _____ Spelling	1st try _____ 2nd try _____ 3rd try _____ Spelling	1st try _____ 2nd try _____ 3rd try _____ Spelling
1st try _____ 2nd try _____ 3rd try _____ Spelling	1st try _____ 2nd try _____ 3rd try _____ Spelling	1st try _____ 2nd try _____ 3rd try _____ Spelling
1st try _____ 2nd try _____ 3rd try _____ Spelling	1st try _____ 2nd try _____ 3rd try _____ Spelling	1st try _____ 2nd try _____ 3rd try _____ Spelling

EDITING MARKS

Correction	Symbol	Example
lowercase	/	She Went to the park.
capitalize	≡	susan has three dogs.
delete	ℓ	Tom likes the the lions.
misspelled word	⬭	Kevin cot the ball. (caught)
new paragraph	¶	John went to sleep late last night. ¶ The next day, John walked to school.
add/insert	∧	We had soup dinner. (for)
move	⟳↗	She ate at the circus cotton candy.
combine two words or parts	‿	I saw some thing.
insert space	#	She likes chocolate icecream.
insert missing punctuation	○	Kelly asked, "Where are you going"

Balancing Literacy © 2001 Creative Teaching Press

EDITING CHECKLIST

Name _____

Date _____

Title _____

❑ I checked for correct punctuation.

❑ I checked for correct capitalization.

❑ I used complete sentences.

❑ I deleted overused words (e.g., then, and, so).

❑ I replaced nonspecific words with more precise words.

❑ I indented each new paragraph.

❑ I circled words that I think may be incorrectly spelled.

❑ I checked the spelling of those words in the dictionary.

❑ I used interesting details to support my ideas.

❑ I gave my edited draft to a partner to check.

❑ I gave my edited draft to my teacher to check.

❑ I completed a Spell-It-Right sheet.

I think my editing skills

❑ are improving   ❑ are the same   ❑ need improvement

Comments:

_____

_____

_____

_____

READER'S REVIEW

Author _____

Title _____

Name:
Comments:

Name:
Comments:

Name:
Comments:

Name:
Comments:

Name:
Comments:

Name:
Comments:

Name:
Comments:

Name:
Comments:

LITERATURE CIRCLES

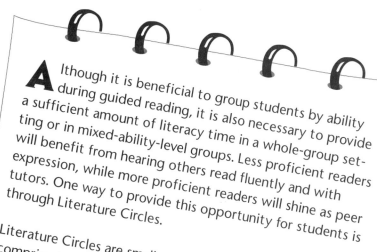

Although it is beneficial to group students by ability during guided reading, it is also necessary to provide a sufficient amount of literacy time in a whole-group setting or in mixed-ability-level groups. Less proficient readers will benefit from hearing others read fluently and with expression, while more proficient readers will shine as peer tutors. One way to provide this opportunity for students is through Literature Circles.

Literature Circles are small, temporary discussion groups comprised of students who have chosen to read the same story, poem, or book. Each group reads a different book, and each member of the group takes on specific responsibilities for group discussions. Discussion topics come from students. They exchange opinions, interpretations, and questions about literature. Students who are reading the same literature gather to discuss the selection and work together to construct meaning from the text. Group meetings aim to be open, natural conversations about books, so encourage personal connections and open-ended questions.

The teacher serves as a facilitator. Most of the teacher's work is organizational and involves collecting sets of appropriate books, helping to form groups, visiting and observing group meetings, conferring with students or groups who struggle, orchestrating sharing sessions, keeping records, and making assessment notes.

Literature Circles offer students the opportunity to become literate. Students begin to think actively and critically about what they read. They become critical thinkers as they engage in ongoing dialogue about their reading.

Student Roles during Literature Circles

Assign each member of a Literature Circle a specific role. The following lists the responsibilities of each role:

SUMMARIZER

Gives a brief summary of the main idea, including the main events.

ILLUSTRATOR

Draws an illustration reflecting the story. Encourage the illustrator to draw a picture of the characters in the story, the setting, a favorite part, a problem, or a prediction.

WORD WIZARD

Reads and displays specific words from the story that may be funny, hard, new, or interesting or that have familiar word chunks in them.

CONNECTOR

Finds connections between the story and real life. This could be the student's own life, someone else's life, or a fictional character's life.

PASSAGE PICKER

Reads aloud several passages from the story to the group. These parts can be scary, confusing, surprising, interesting, or funny or teach a moral lesson.

DISCUSSION DIRECTOR

Poses questions for the group to discuss. These questions are related to the story in some way.

Introducing Literature Circles

When introducing Literature Circles, provide plenty of guidance and modeling. Make sure students have a thorough understanding of how Literature Circles work before having them work independently in their groups. The following provides a sample of how Literature Circles can be introduced to the class. This entire orientation process may take about two weeks, depending upon your class and teaching style.

DAY 1

Introduce the term Literature Circle, and invite students to consider what it might be. Record their ideas, and incorporate them into your explanation of the activity. Read a short story to the class, and then conduct a whole-group Literature Circle. Invite students to comment on, question, and discuss what was read.

DAY 2

Explain and model the role of the Summarizer. Discuss the story that was read on day 1. Encourage students to brainstorm a list of the main events from the story. Give each student a Summarizer Task Sheet (page 95). Have students write a summary of the story's main idea. Divide the class into groups of six. Encourage students to discuss their summary with the rest of their group. Bring the class together as a whole group to share their small-group discussions.

DAY 3

Explain the role of the Illustrator. Discuss how the illustrator responds to the literature with a graphic rather than in words. Lead a discussion on the importance of pictures and visuals in books. Give each student an Illustrator Task Sheet (page 96) and another short story. Have students read the story and illustrate a picture based on the story. Then, ask them to meet with their Literature Circles and discuss the illustrations with their group. Bring the class together again, and invite volunteers to share their pictures.

DAY 4

Explain the role of the Word Wizard. Help students find noteworthy words in the previous day's reading. Give each student a Word Wizard Task Sheet (page 97) and another short story. Have students read the story and take the role of Word Wizard. After the class has had time to record their words on the task sheet, invite students to discuss any problems they may have had.

DAY 5

Explain the role of the Connector. Discuss with the class how the previous day's reading relates to something in their lives. Give each student a Connector Task Sheet (page 98). Have students complete their sheet. Have them meet in their Literature Circles and discuss their answers with the rest of their group. Meet as a class again, and invite volunteers to share their answers.

DAY 6

Explain the role of the Passage Picker. Give each student another short story, and model how to choose a passage from the story. Give each child a Passage Picker Task Sheet (page 99), and explain how to fill it out. Show students how to use bookmarks or sticky notes to mark the pages on which the passages appear. Have students meet in their Literature Circles and practice the role of Passage Picker. Meet as a class again, and invite volunteers to share the passages they chose. Further discuss the process of locating passages if necessary.

DAY 7

Model the role of the Discussion Director. Explain what open-ended questions are. Have students think of questions about the story from the previous day. Point out how some questions can be answered in one or two words while others have many different answers and can lead to a discussion. Give each student a Discussion Director Task Sheet (page 100) and a short story. Have students read the story, and encourage them to write two to three open-ended questions based on their reading. Have them meet in their Literature Circles to share and discuss their questions. Meet as a class again to review questions or comments from the small groups.

Assessment

Use the Literature Circle Evaluation Form (page 101) to record individual student progress. Give a copy of the form to each student. Have students circle either +, ✓, or − for each statement in the student column. Have them circle the + if the statement is always true, ✓ if the statement is sometimes true, and − if the statement is never true. Encourage students to complete the two statements at the bottom of the page. Collect the forms, and complete the column entitled *Teacher* on each student's form. Conference with each student to discuss and compare opinions.

Use the Group Assessment Checklist (page 102) to evaluate each group's progress. List the group members' names along with the date of their first meeting and their book title or topic of discussion. Check off each task as the group completes it.

Monitor students' participation on the Participation Record reproducible (page 103). List each group member's name, and draw a tally mark next to the name of students who participate in the group's discussion. Note any observations you make (e.g., needs to participate more) by jotting them down in the Comments section.

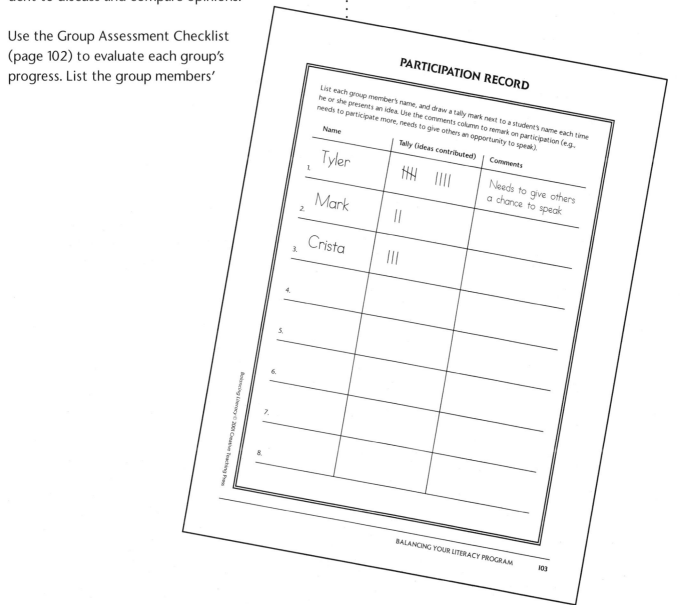

PARTICIPATION RECORD

List each group member's name, and draw a tally mark next to a student's name each time he or she presents an idea. Use the comments column to remark on participation (e.g., needs to participate more, needs to give others an opportunity to speak).

Name	Tally (ideas contributed)	Comments
1. Tyler	ℋℋ ‖‖	Needs to give others a chance to speak
2. Mark	‖	
3. Crista	‖‖	
4.		
5.		
6.		
7.		
8.		

BALANCING YOUR LITERACY PROGRAM

103

LITERATURE CIRCLES SCHEDULE

8:45–9:00	MORNING BUSINESS, JOURNAL WRITING
9:00–9:20	MINI-LESSON
9:20–9:50	LITERATURE CIRCLES (15-MINUTE GROUP MEETING AND DISCUSSION, 15 MINUTES FOR READING AND TASK SHEETS)
9:50–10:05	RECESS
10:05–10:20	MINI-LESSON (WRITING SKILLS)
10:20–11:20	WRITING CENTER AND SPELLING CENTER, TEACHER WORKS WITH STUDENTS WHO NEED GUIDED READING LESSON
11:20–12:00	MATH
12:00–12:45	LUNCH
12:45–1:00	SUSTAINED SILENT READING
1:00–2:00	SOCIAL STUDIES/SCIENCE
2:00–2:30	PHYSICAL EDUCATION
2:30–2:45	TEACHER READ-ALOUD
2:45–3:00	CLASS NEWS, CLEANUP

How the schedule incorporates the literacy components

LITERACY COMPONENT	ACTIVITY
Modeled Reading	teacher read-aloud
Shared Reading	Literature Circles
Guided Reading	teacher-led center
Independent Reading	Literature Circles, Sustained Silent Reading
Interactive Writing	Class News
Modeled or Shared Writing	mini-lesson
Guided Writing	mini-lesson
Independent Writing	Literature Circles, Writing Center

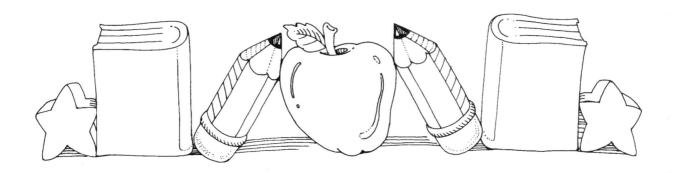

SUMMARIZER TASK SHEET

Name _____

Date _____

Other Group Members

_____

_____

Book Title

_____

Task: Write a brief summary of the story. Include the main events.

_____

_____

_____

_____

_____

_____

_____

_____

_____

_____

_____

ILLUSTRATOR TASK SHEET

Name _____

Date _____

Other Group Members

_____

_____

Book Title

_____

Task: Draw a picture relating to the story. You can illustrate characters, the setting, a problem, your favorite part, or a prediction of what will happen next in the story.

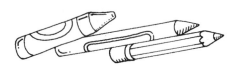
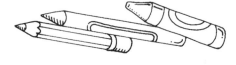

Balancing Literacy © 2001 Creative Teaching Press

WORD WIZARD TASK SHEET

Name _____

Date _____

Other Group Members

_____

_____

Book Title

_____

Task: Find six interesting, powerful, or funny words from today's reading. Write the words below. Write the page number each word is on and the reason you chose it. Use bookmarks to mark the pages on which the words appear in the book.

Word	Page Number	Reason for Choosing the Word
1.		
2.		
3.		
4.		
5.		
6.		

CONNECTOR TASK SHEET

Name _____

Date _____

Other Group Members

_____

_____

Book Title

_____

Task: Find connections between the story and real life. Use the following questions to help.

Have you ever felt like a character in this story? When?

_____

_____

Have you ever visited a place like the one in this story? Explain.

_____

_____

Has anything ever happened to you that is similar to a situation in this story? Explain.

_____

_____

How does this book remind you of another book you've read?

_____

_____

PASSAGE PICKER TASK SHEET

Name _____

Date _____

Other Group Members

_____

_____

Book Title

_____

Task: Choose three interesting passages to read aloud to your group. Choose passages that are important to the story (e.g., the story would change if that part were deleted). Write the passages below. Write the page number each passage is on and the reason you chose it. Use bookmarks to mark the pages on which the passages appear in the book.

First Sentence of Passage	Page Number	Reason for Choosing This Passage
1.		
2.		
3.		

DISCUSSION DIRECTOR TASK SHEET

Name _____

Date _____

Other Group Members

_____

_____

Book Title

_____

Task: Write three questions about what you read. These questions
should initiate group discussion. Choose questions that will result
in reactions and concerns from group members.

1. _____

_____

_____

2. _____

_____

_____

3. _____

_____

_____

LITERATURE CIRCLE EVALUATION FORM

Student _____ Date _____

Book/Topic _____

	Student			Teacher		
Preparation						
Completed reading	+	✓	−	+	✓	−
Completed task sheet	+	✓	−	+	✓	−
Participation						
Shared ideas and offered suggestions	+	✓	−	+	✓	−
Stayed on topic and helped the group stay focused	+	✓	−	+	✓	−
Made eye contact	+	✓	−	+	✓	−
Listened to others	+	✓	−	+	✓	−
Encouraged others to speak	+	✓	−	+	✓	−
Disagreed without hurting others' feelings	+	✓	−	+	✓	−

My most important contribution to the discussions was _____

_____.

My plan for improvement is _____

_____.

GROUP ASSESSMENT CHECKLIST

Group Members

_____

_____

_____

Book/Topic _____

Date _____

❑   Literature Circle Evaluation

❑   Task Sheets

❑   Extension activity

❑   Student-teacher conference

❑   Observations/Observational log

❑   Group interview

❑   Class presentation

❑   Participation

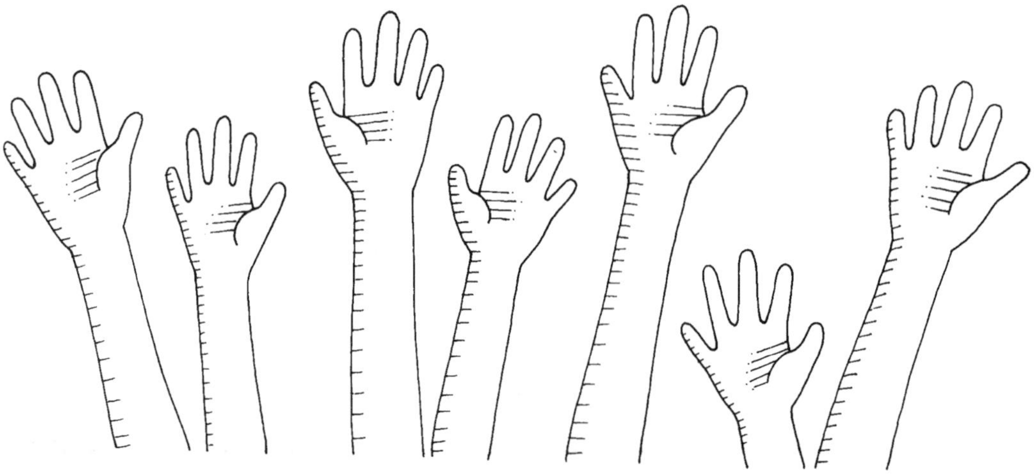

PARTICIPATION RECORD

List each group member's name, and draw a tally mark next to a student's name each time he or she presents an idea. Use the comments column to remark on participation (e.g., needs to participate more, needs to give others an opportunity to speak).

Name	Tally (ideas contributed)	Comments
1.		
2.		
3.		
4.		
5.		
6.		
7.		
8.		

LITERACY CENTERS

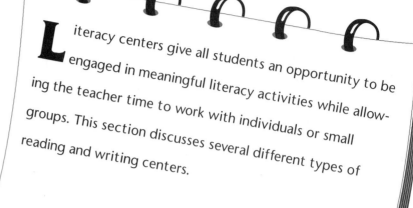

Literacy centers give all students an opportunity to be engaged in meaningful literacy activities while allowing the teacher time to work with individuals or small groups. This section discusses several different types of reading and writing centers.

ARRANGING THE CENTERS

Consider the following factors when setting up literacy centers:
- the size of the room
- availability of materials and furniture
- types/kinds of centers to set up
- permanent vs. moveable centers

If your classroom space is limited, you can make mobile centers using boxes, cans, folders, envelopes, and resealable plastic bags. The mobile centers require very little storage or display space. You can easily move them from one area of the room to another. Students can use these centers at their desk or take them home. For centers that require more materials, like the writing center, have all the writing materials in a bin or box that can be easily moved and stored. If you do not have room for a reading center, have a bookcase with several books where students can make their reading selections. Then, have students sit at their desk or a quiet place in the room to read their book.

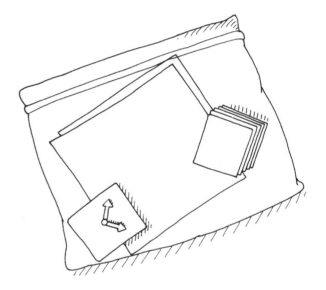

HOW TO MANAGE CENTERS

- Assign students to a group.
- Rotate groups through centers.
- Use the Center Contract (page 110) for students to choose their center schedule for the week.
- Decide on the amount of time for center use.
- Devise a chart or planning board to manage center rotations.

Planning Boards

Planning boards can be designed for small-group rotations or for managing individual use at centers. There are several ways to make a planning board. Here are just two possibilities.

SMALL-GROUP USE

For small-group use, have three to four rotations per day. Have each group at one center per rotation. To make a small-group planning board, draw a grid on a large piece of poster board. Make a row for each group, and list the group name at the left of each row. Attach a Velcro piece in each square of the grid. Make cutouts that will fit into the squares. Label each cutout with a center name. Assign each group a different center for each allotted time slot. Include one symbol cutout labeled *Free Choice* for each group.

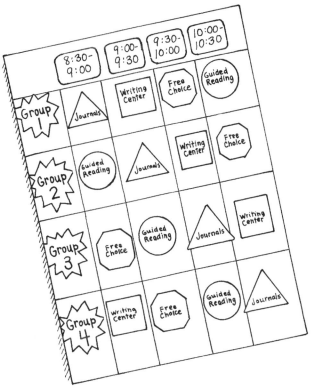

INDIVIDUAL USE

For managing individual use at centers, the planning board serves as a way to make sure there are not too many students at one center. For example, if you have three spots for the Listening Center on the board, that means that only three students can be at the Listening Center at the same time. To make an individual-use planning board, write the titles of your centers on separate sentence strips, and glue them to a large piece of poster board. Use a razor blade to make slits beneath each title, and place a paper clip in each slit. Make as many slits as you want spaces at each center. For example, if you want to allow three people at the Library Center, make three slits under the title *Library*. Label a cutout for each student. Have students choose a center and place their name card in the correct place on the planning board.

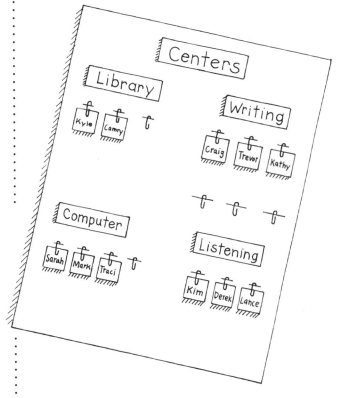

CENTERS SCHEDULE

The time you schedule for centers will depend on the needs of your students. Adapt the following schedule to work with your daily classroom routine and curriculum goals.

7:45–8:00	MORNING BUSINESS, JOURNAL WRITING
8:00–10:00	LITERACY LEARNING CENTERS (3 GROUPS, 40-MINUTE ROTATIONS) • GUIDED READING/WRITING WITH TEACHER • WRITING CENTER • FREE CHOICE
10:00–10:15	RECESS
10:15–11:00	MATH
11:00–12:00	SOCIAL STUDIES/SCIENCE
12:00–12:45	LUNCH
12:45–1:00	SUSTAINED SILENT READING
1:00–1:30	PHYSICAL EDUCATION
1:30–1:45	DAILY NEWS
1:45–2:00	TEACHER READ-ALOUD
2:00–2:15	CLEANUP

How the schedule incorporates the literacy components

LITERACY COMPONENT	ACTIVITY
Modeled Reading	teacher read-aloud
Shared Reading	Listening Center
Guided Reading	Literacy Center, teacher-led group
Independent Reading	Library Center, Sustained Silent Reading
Interactive Writing	Class News (teacher and students write text)
Modeled or Shared Writing	Class News (teacher writes text)
Guided Writing	Literacy Center, teacher-led group
Independent Writing	Writing Center, Post Office Center, journals

Reading and Writing Centers

There are many literacy centers you can use to have students practice their reading and writing skills. This section provides ideas for centers, including a list of suggested materials and activities for each center. Adapt or add to these ideas to create a collection of centers that works best in your classroom.

WRITING CENTER

Materials

writing tools (e.g., pencils, pens), paper, dictionary, thesaurus, writing/editing tips charts, writing topic ideas

- Sticker Stories
  Create "sticker story cards" by placing a sticker on each of several index cards. Have students choose a card and write a story about the sticker. Ask them to write directly on the front and back of the card. The stories can be real or imaginary.

- Picture Prompts
  Cut out magazine pictures or take real photographs, and glue each picture on a separate index card. Have students choose a picture and write a story about it. The stories can be real or imaginary.

- Dialogue Journal
  Set up a notebook with an initial message from you. Invite students to share their opinions or respond to what was written. Encourage students to write freely. If you notice any common misspellings, model these words in your responses.

- Comic Strips
  Cut out several comic strips, and use paper or correction fluid to cover or delete the text in the speech bubbles. Make copies of the comic strips for students, and invite them to write their own text in each bubble.

- Discussion Box
  Place a container labeled *Discussion Box* at the center. Have students think of a topic they would like to discuss in class and write it on a piece of paper. They may include a paragraph on their opinion of the subject or reasons why they would like to bring it up. Set aside time each week or take advantage of extra time to choose a topic out of the Discussion Box to become the focus of a conversation or a writing assignment.

LIBRARY CENTER

Materials

bookshelves, books, pillows, comfy chairs or beanbags

- Have students independently read books of their choice. Encourage them to write in a literary journal each time they finish a book.

SPELLING CENTER

Materials

rubber stamps, markers, word searches, pencils, chalk/chalkboard, paper

- Encourage students to use rubber stamps or markers to write their spelling words, or have them use the words to make word searches.

POETRY CENTER

Materials

poetry books, laminated poems, class-written poems (display various types of poems as a reference)

- Make a poetry anthology book for each student by binding several sheets of paper together. Display copies of different poems. Have students glue a poem on a left-hand page of their book and respond to the poem on the facing page. Invite students to write or illustrate their response.

COMPUTER CENTER

Materials

computers, reference charts (e.g., parts of the computer or how to use the computer), software

- Make a computer log for each student by binding several sheets of paper together. Invite students to practice literacy skills by using appropriate educational software (see page 127). Have students write down the program they used and three things they learned in their computer log. If you have Internet access, students can play interactive literacy games (see page 127) or research information on the Web.

LISTENING CENTER

Materials

cassette players and headsets, cassette tapes with corresponding books

• Invite students to listen to books on tape. Provide professional recordings or recordings and books made by your students.

DRAMA CENTER

Materials

scarves, dress-up clothing, other props, writing supplies, art supplies

• Invite students to write plays or skits. Encourage students to create scenery and props for their skits. Have students rehearse their acts and perform them for the rest of the class.

POST OFFICE CENTER

Materials

stationery, paper, envelopes, pretend stamps, pencils

• Invite students to write a letter to a pen pal, a classmate, a teacher, a family member, an author, or the school principal. Have students address an envelope and put their written letter in it. Encourage them to place a pretend stamp on the envelope and place it in the class mailbox. Select a student to be a mail carrier who is responsible for delivering the letters to the proper people in school. If the letter is addressed to someone outside of school, have the carrier give the letter to the sender to mail out.

CENTER CONTRACT

For the week of _____

Name _____

This week I plan to accomplish the following:

-
-
-
-
-
-
-
-
-

I reached my goal for the week. _____

Signature

I did not reach my goal this week because _____ .

Assessment

ome teachers assign a spelling list and give weekly tests of the words. Others may find it more beneficial to note observations of student progress by reading students' journals or stories. There is an endless numbers of ways to assess students: tests, observations, checklists, rubrics, interviews, the list goes on. Knowing what information you want to get will help you choose the types of assessments to use.

This section explains various assessment methods and strategies, including ways to assess your students' progress in reading, writing, spelling, and phonics. This section features numerous assessment reproducibles. You can use the reproducibles as they are or alter them to fit your specific assessment needs. They can also be used as examples to follow when creating your own assessment sheets.

It is important to assess your students throughout the year, not only to note their progress but also to determine if you need to alter your program.

TYPES OF ASSESSMENT

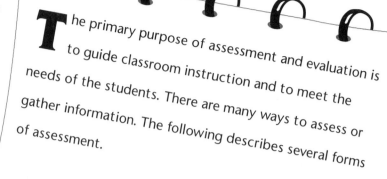

The primary purpose of assessment and evaluation is to guide classroom instruction and to meet the needs of the students. There are many ways to assess or gather information. The following describes several forms of assessment.

AUTHENTIC ASSESSMENT

Students perform meaningful tasks as a form of assessment. The process that students take in completing a task is just as important as their final product. For authentic assessment, students could

- read real text
- write about meaningful topics
- discuss books
- keep journals
- write letters
- revise their own writing

Performance assessment requires students to demonstrate their knowledge, skills, and strategies by creating a response. Formats range from short answers to long-term projects. For performance assessment, students could

- conduct and write a research report
- develop a character analysis
- create a mobile
- draw and write about a story
- read aloud a personally meaningful section of a story

Ongoing assessment uses more than just one sample of students' abilities. The teacher keeps a collection of work samples (throughout the school year) for each student. Ongoing assessment shows you the growth in each student's learning and documents both achievement and growth. An example of ongoing assessment is a portfolio.

FORMAL ASSESSMENT

This approach provides the teacher with a systematic way to evaluate each student's progress (e.g., standard testing).

INFORMAL ASSESSMENT

This approach gives students the opportunity to demonstrate what they know in situations that are familiar to them. There are two methods of informal assessment:

- Observation and recording—keep notes, anecdotal records, checklists, or a rating scale
- Collection and analysis—keep samples of each student's work (e.g., journals, essays, reports, reading logs, group or individual projects)

When you are reviewing your observations and other collected data, it's important to have an organized system to document academic growth.

Rubrics are one method of organizing informal assessment. Refer to the sample reading and writing rubrics on pages 114 and 115. One shows four categories, while the other shows six categories. Evaluate your district or school's grading scale before determining what type of rubric you are going to use. If your school's report card uses a six-category rubric scale, then develop a six-category rubric for evaluating your class. If your school uses a traditional letter grading system, develop a five-category rubric. This will make it easier to transfer a rubric rating to a letter grade if necessary (e.g., 5 = A, 4 = B, 3 = C, 2 = D, 1 = F). Rubrics can also be used to assess spelling (see page 116).

When designing your own rubric, keep the following suggestions in mind:

- Design rubrics that have guidelines for observation, assessment, and evaluation.
- Create rubrics that value the students' process as well as the final product.
- Evaluate students' literacy performance and progress based on each student's progress and achievement.

STUDENT SELF-ASSESSMENT

In this approach, students compare their own work over time, create evaluation criteria for a project, discuss their strategies, work with peers to evaluate and revise pieces of writing, and review their reading logs. Have students complete a Self-Assessment reproducible (page 117) to reflect on one of their work samples. When students participate in the evaluation process, they develop the habit of self-reflection. They learn the qualities of good work, how to judge their work against these qualities, and how to set personal goals.

READING RUBRIC

6 = Exceptional Reader
Reads and understands advanced materials
Enjoys independently pursuing own interests
Can summarize concisely
Makes inferences and uses text to support ideas
Uses wide range of strategies to deal with difficult tasks

5 = Strong Reader
Reads and understands books appropriate for grade level and above
Reads during silent reading
Independently selects appropriate books
Can summarize what was read
Makes inferences
Has strategies to deal with unfamiliar material

4 = Capable Reader
Reads and understands grade-appropriate books
Selects appropriate books independently
Can retell a story
Begins to make inferences
Uses reading strategies for meaning

3 = Developing Reader
Reads and understands short books
Relies on rereading familiar books
Needs help reading and understanding grade-appropriate books

2 = Limited Reader
Reads and understands easy and familiar material
Has difficulty with unfamiliar material
Rarely reads for pleasure
Sometimes uses reading strategies

1 = Emergent Reader
Needs support in all areas
Rarely uses reading strategies

Balancing Literacy © 2001 Creative Teaching Press

WRITING RUBRIC

Name _____ Date _____

Student's score = _____+_____+_____+_____+_____+_____+_____+_____=_____
                      A   B   C   D   E   F   G   H   total

_____/8 =_____=_____
total   score   rounded score

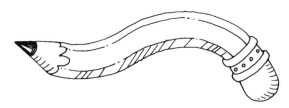

	Strong—4	Capable—3	Developing—2	Limited—1
A. Organization	Clear beginning, middle, and ending with ideas smoothly connected	Logical sequencing with some gaps between transitions	Inconsistent organization, lacking transitions	No story organization
B. Relevance	All sentences are related to the topic, story remains focused	Most sentences are related to the topic, story is generally focused	Topic is addressed, but loses focus at times	Topic is not addressed and there is no focus
C. Elaboration	Writer uses imaginative details and fully developed ideas	Writer successfully communicates ideas using some details	Writer attempts to develop very basic ideas, but doesn't get specific enough	Writer's ideas are undeveloped
D. Vocabulary	Writer uses a wide variety of descriptive and appropriate vocabulary	Writer uses some variety of vocabulary with occasional weak or misused words	Writer uses vague, repetitious, or misused vocabulary most of the time	Writer uses ineffective vocabulary
E. Sentence Patterns	Writer uses varied sentence patterns throughout	Writer uses some variety of sentence patterns	Writer uses only short and patterned sentences	Writer doesn't form complete sentences
F. Mechanics	Writer uses standard application of punctuation and capitalization most of the time	Writer uses standard application of punctuation and capitalization some of the time	Writer rarely uses standard application of punctuation and capitalization	Writer never uses standard application of punctuation and capitalization
G. Spelling	Writer mostly uses conventional spelling	Writer uses more conventional spelling than temporary spelling; spelling errors don't interfere with the reading and meaning	Writer uses mostly temporary spelling that can be understood at times	Writer has many spelling errors that interfere with the reading and meaning
H. Content Originality	Content is highly original, creative elements (e.g., dialogue, suspense) are used	Content is original	Content is very predictable most of the time	Originality is not evident

SPELLING DEVELOPMENT RUBRIC

Spelling tests are one way to evaluate students' spelling progress. However, students must apply what they learned to their writing in order to be considered proficient spellers. Use the following rubric to evaluate students' spelling progress. Combine how often students use spelling skills in their writing with their spelling test average to calulate a report card grade.

Use of Spelling Skills in Writing +	Spelling Test Average =	Report Card Grade
All of the time	100%+	A
Most of the time Some of the time Most of the time	90–100% 90–100% 75–89%	B
Some of the time Most of the time	75–89% 60–74%	C
Some of the time	60–74%	D
Some of the time Never	Below 60%	F

Balancing Literacy © 2001 Creative Teaching Press

SELF-ASSESSMENT

Name _____

I chose this work, _____,

because _____.

These are the things that I did well:

-

-

-

These are the things that I would like to improve on:

-

-

-

This is what I learned:

-

-

-

ASSESSMENT METHODS

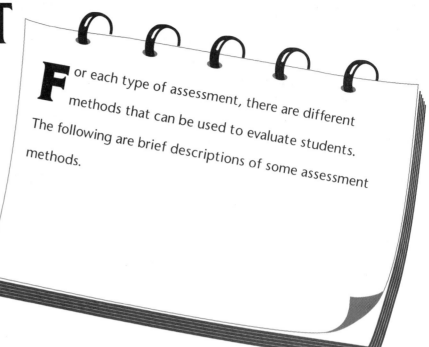

For each type of assessment, there are different methods that can be used to evaluate students. The following are brief descriptions of some assessment methods.

ANECDOTAL RECORDS

Make quick, informal observations to note each student's behavior. Anecdotal records are kept for student's records and for planning purposes. Place several copies of the Anecdotal Record reproducible (page 120) on a clipboard, and carry it as you observe students reading, writing, and interacting with each other. Record observations. Keep completed records in a binder, or put each record in the corresponding student's portfolio. For example, write *Kristen used editing marks when proofing her story* on the anecdotal record. Cut apart the strip containing these comments, and place it in Kristen's portfolio.

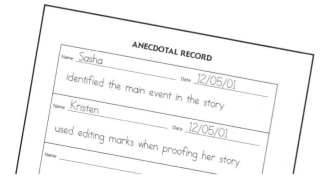

CONFERENCES

Use conferences to assess, collaborate with, and guide students. There are several types of conferences, including reading, writing, goal setting, and evaluation (e.g., portfolio conferences, see page 48).

CHECKLISTS

Use checklists to quickly note the traits or skills you observe students demonstrating. Make checklists based on criteria for given projects or tasks, or create them to cover broader areas like reading and writing. See the Writing Checklist (page 121).

KWHL CHARTS

Use a KWHL chart to assess what students know, what they want to learn, how they can find out what they want to learn, and what they learned. Have each student fill out a KWHL Chart (page 122) throughout the stages of a lesson. In the beginning of a lesson, the chart serves as a written record of the students' prior knowledge (K) and allows students to note what they want to learn (W) and how they would go about finding that information (H). Following the lesson, have students self-assess what they learned (L).

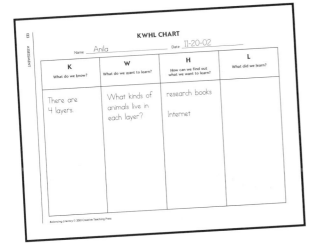

INVESTIGATIONS

Investigations may relate to a specific subject area or involve several areas, integrating the curriculum. Forms of investigation are a collection of student writing, graphs, charts, experiments, and other products. When students are involved in these investigations, they are often not even aware that they are being assessed.

PRODUCTS

Students demonstrate understanding, application, originality, and organizational skills in making a final product. Products can be in the form of writing, videotapes, audiotapes, dramatic performances, bulletin boards, or computer demonstrations.

RESPONSE GROUPS

Response groups are opportunities for small groups of students to discuss books or events in depth with one another (e.g., Literature Circles). By observing students in a response group, you will gain insight into their thinking skills.

INVENTORIES

Inventories show a student's progress over time. An inventory consists of a list of skills or strategies that helps to direct your observations of the student. Use an inventory to easily record your observations throughout the school year. Copy the Reading Inventory reproducible (page 123), or create your own.

LEARNING LOGS

A learning log is a type of journal that enables students to write across the curriculum. Use learning logs to encourage students to be in control of their own learning and to promote thinking through writing.

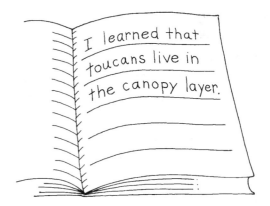

INTERVIEWS

In interviews, students respond to single questions or questions asked by you. Interviews provide an opportunity for you to determine a student's depth of understanding rather than whether the student can provide the "correct" answer.

ANECDOTAL RECORD

Name _____ Date _____

Name _____ Date _____

Name _____ Date _____

Name _____ Date _____

Name _____ Date _____

Name _____ Date _____

Balancing Literacy © 2001 Creative Teaching Press

WRITING CHECKLIST

Name _____ Date _____

Conventions

❑ Sentences are complete
❑ Handwriting is legible
❑ Sentences go from left to right
❑ Sentences build upon the ones before them
❑ Each paragraph has one main idea

Punctuation and Capitalization

❑ Uses ending punctuation
❑ Uses commas
❑ Uses quotation marks in dialogue
❑ Properly uses apostrophes
  and exclamation marks
❑ Uses correct capitalization

Grammar

❑ Uses verb tense agreement throughout writing
❑ Uses subject/predicate agreement
❑ Uses paragraphs
❑ Uses figure of speech

Resources

❑ Uses the dictionary to spell unknown words
❑ Uses a thesaurus to find synonyms for overused words

Ideas

❑ Uses brainstorming or a story map
  to create and organize ideas
❑ Writes a story with a beginning,
  a middle, and an end
❑ Includes a satisfying conclusion

KWHL CHART

Name _____ Date _____

K What do we <u>k</u>now?	W What do we <u>w</u>ant to learn?	H <u>H</u>ow can we find out what we want to learn?	L What did we <u>l</u>earn?

Balancing Literacy © 2001 Creative Teaching Press

READING INVENTORY

Name _____

	Date	Date	Date	Date
Integrates reading strategies and cross checks cueing systems				
Uses reading strategies for familiar text				
Uses reading strategies for unfamiliar text				
Has a large sight word vocabulary				
Reads independently				
Chooses appropriate reading materials				
Responds to literature from different points of views				
Reads informational books				
Reads for meaning				
Reads a variety of sources to research projects				
Is capable of reading different kinds of text across the curriculum				
Has developed a personal taste in fiction or nonfiction books				

PORTFOLIOS

A portfolio is a meaningful collection of a student's work. Both the student and teacher select work samples. A portfolio often displays the student's best work, but it can also include drafts, the student's self-assessment (see page 117), or types of work that highlight the process the student took to complete a task. Portfolios should reflect the day-to-day learning activities of students. Add samples to portfolios on an ongoing basis so they accurately reflect the students' progress and achievements over time.

THINGS TO INCLUDE IN A PORTFOLIO

- student process samples (e.g., first draft of a story)
- student product samples (e.g., published story)
- teacher observations (e.g., anecdotal notes)
- information gathered through assessment and evaluation strategies (e.g., checklists, rubrics, learning logs, KWHL charts)
- student and parent comments (e.g., For the Portfolio reproducible, see page 125)

FOR THE PORTFOLIO

Name _____ Date _____

Student Comments

I chose this work because _____

_____

_____

_____

Parent Comments

_____

_____

_____

_____

Teacher Comments

_____

_____

_____

_____

Integrating Technology

It is essential for students to understand and experience technology as they prepare for their future. Have students learn and practice literacy skills with various software programs. Teach them how to create multi-media presentations in place of standard book reports or research reports. Students who can access and "surf" the Internet obtain information on a wealth of topics. The Internet also features many interactive games that provide students with fun and interesting ways to learn literacy skills. Refer to the suggested list of Literacy Software Programs and Web sites on page 127.

LITERACY SOFTWARE PROGRAMS

The Clue Finders–Reading Adventures
(The Learning Company)
Students solve the mystery of the missing amulet while developing confidence in reading comprehension, spelling, grammar, and critical thinking.

Reader Blaster 3rd Grade (Havas Interactive)
Students practice sentence structure, label parts of speech, apply grammar skills, understand analogies, and find synonyms and antonyms. There are also Reader Blaster software programs for 4th and 5th grades.

Leap Ahead Spelling Ages 7–12
(The Learning Company)
Students practice spelling skills, word recognition, critical thinking skills, word recall, and language development.

Storybook Weaver Deluxe (The Learning Company)
Students will be involved in the learning process and will improve their writing skills by using this program. Students illustrate stories using the provided graphics or use the graphics to give them ideas for a story.

Schoolhouse Rock Grammar Pack
(The Learning Company)
Students participate in activities to improve reading skills, expand their vocabulary, and build writing confidence. Activities are based on the Schoolhouse Rock parts of speech songs.

INTERACTIVE LITERACY GAMES

The following sites were found to be functional, child friendly, and child safe at the time of publication, but all sites should be checked by a responsible adult before directing students to them.

Fun Brain at **www.funbrain.com**
This site has several interactive literacy games—Grammar Gorillas, Reading Instruments, and Vocabulary and Spelling games.

Children's Story at **www.childrenstory.com**
Here students can read a story or have a story read to them. Stories include fairy tales, holiday stories, and interactive stories.

Vocabulary at **www.vocabulary.com**
Students can practice vocabulary by doing a fill-in-the-blank game or definition matching.

Wacky Web Tales at **www.eduplace.com/tales**
Students create their own stories by inserting parts of speech into a story frame.

Grammar Bytes at **www.chompchomp.com**
This site provides students with an interactive grammar review. Topics include comma splices and fused sentences, irregular verbs, and correct usage of "lay" vs. "lie."

Teacher Resource Books

Reading

Direct Reading Instruction by Douglas W. Carnine, Jerry Silbert, and Edward J. Kameehui (Prentice Hall)

Getting Started with Literature Circles by Katherine L. Schlick Noe and Nancy Johnson (Christopher-Gordon Publishing)

Guided Reading: Good First Teaching for all Children by Irene Fountas and Gay Su Pinnell (Heinemann)

Literature Circles: Voice and Choice in the Student-Centered Classroom by Harvey Daniels (Stenhouse Publishing)

Mosaic of Thought: Teaching Comprehension in a Reader's Workshop by Ellin Oliver Keene and Susan Zimmermann (Heinemann)

The Read-Aloud Handbook by Jim Trelease (Penguin USA)

Writing

The Art of Teaching Writing by Lucy McCormick-Calkins (Heinemann)

A Fresh Look at Writing by Donald Graves (Heinemann)

Teaching Writing: Balancing Process and Product by Gail E. Tompkins (Merrill Publishing)

Spelling and Phonics

Ideas for Spelling by F. Bolton and D. Snowball (Heinemann)

Teaching Kids to Spell by Richard R. Gentry and Jean Wallace Gillet (Heinemann)

Word Journeys Assessment—Guided Phonics, Spelling, and Vocabulary Instruction by Kathy Ganske (Guilford Press)

Word Matters: Teaching Phonics and Spelling in the Reading/Writing Classroom by Gay Su Pinnell and Irene C. Fountas (Heinemann)

Words Their Way: Word Study for Phonics, Vocabulary, and Spelling Instruction by Donald R. Bear (Prentice Hall)

Assessment

Authentic Reading Assessment: Practices and Possibilities by Sheila W. Valencia, Elfrieda H. Hiebert, and Peter P. Afflerbach (International Reading Association)

Literacy Assessment: A Handbook of Instruments by Lynn K. Rhodes (Heinemann)

Running Records for Classroom Teachers by Marie M. Clay (Heinemann)